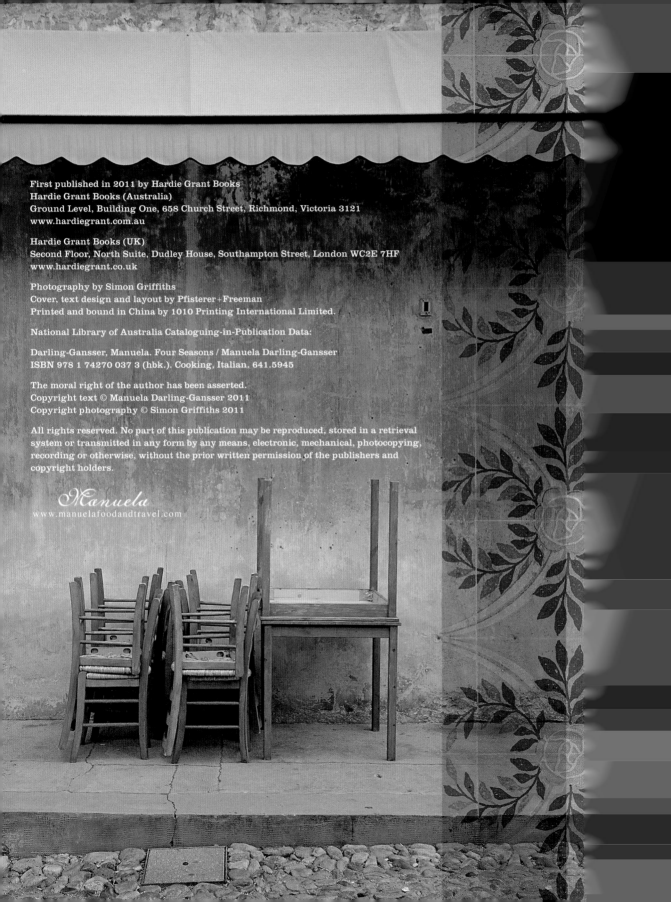

First published in 2011 by Hardie Grant Books
Hardie Grant Books (Australia)
Ground Level, Building One, 658 Church Street, Richmond, Victoria 3121
www.hardiegrant.com.au

Hardie Grant Books (UK)
Second Floor, North Suite, Dudley House, Southampton Street, London WC2E 7HF
www.hardiegrant.co.uk

Photography by Simon Griffiths
Cover, text design and layout by Pfisterer+Freeman
Printed and bound in China by 1010 Printing International Limited.

National Library of Australia Cataloguing-in-Publication Data:

Darling-Gansser, Manuela. Four Seasons / Manuela Darling-Gansser
ISBN 978 1 74270 037 3 (hbk.). Cooking, Italian. 641.5945

Manuela
www.manuelafoodandtravel.com

Four Seasons

A Year of Italian Food

MANUELA DARLING-GANSSER

Photography by Simon Griffiths

hardie grant books

MELBOURNE · LONDON

Per Miranda, Jason e Birri

CONTENTS

A YEAR OF ITALIAN FOOD

A defining characteristic of traditional Italian food is that it is strongly seasonal. Favoured ingredients are available in some seasons but not in others, and every season seems to have its culinary stars. Also, certain dishes are customarily prepared at particular times of the year. You can break the rules, of course, but it is widely understood by people in Italy (who take their cooking and eating seriously – and isn't that just about everyone?) that there is definitely a right time to eat certain foods if you want them at their very best.

In other cuisines seasonality may not be so strong, particularly in those countries nearer the tropics where they don't have the four seasons – maybe two at best: the wet and the dry. You don't hear about spring food in Thailand or autumn food in Canton.

Seasonality in Italy is often combined with a strong sense of place. The country has a very varied geography, from the Alps in the north, the Po River Valley at their feet, a long mountain chain down the spine of a narrow peninsula stretching far down into the Mediterranean, an extended coastline and numerous islands, two of which – Sardinia and Sicily – are large with mountainous interiors. It's a country tailor-made for a wide range of micro-climates, extremes of weather and significant differences between one place and another at various times of the year.

It is for this reason that when you talk about seasons in Italy you end up talking about regions as well. Spring comes early in Sicily while Piemonte in the north-west may still be under snow. People have strong views about which region is best in a particular season and, being Italy, these views can be very different. Ultimately it's a matter of personal taste. The links between seasons and locations I have chosen for this book reflect very much my preferences and the association I have with various places. So for me winter is all about the Alps, as summer is about beaches and the sea. My family comes from Lugano in the Italian-speaking south of Switzerland, just north of Milan. We used to go into the mountains in winter and to the island of Sardinia in the summer. So the recipes I have chosen for winter and summer reflect these places as well as the seasons.

My choice for autumn is Piemonte, an area not far from Lugano. It is the home of some of the great ingredients of Italian cooking – porcini mushrooms, risotto rices, white truffles, mountain cheeses and famous wines – all of which are at their seasonal peak in autumn.

Spring for me means Sicily, the first region to experience the new season's warmth. Spring is also, in food terms, the best time to be in Sicily. Summers are hot, autumns parched, winters a bit bleak, but in spring the abundance the island produces is all on show.

You might ask, why the emphasis now on seasonality when many ingredients are available year-round, imported if necessary? For the many people who live in cities rather than the countryside, seasonal difference may not be availability, simply price.

I am not a complete purist on this. There are times when I do use out-of-season ingredients but I see this as the exception rather than the rule. For me the heart of the matter comes down to authenticity, the integrity of the food. In-season ingredients from the right region should always be your preference for one simple reason – they taste better. If you want to enjoy food that is varied, right for the timeof year and the best possible expression of the taste and goodness of the ingredients themselves, then you must eat seasonally. Anything else is a second-rate experience!

This book is a guide to my favourite seasonal Italian recipes and the regions that inspire them. It's a very personal choice but, as you try these recipes, you will enjoy a very varied range of some of the best cooking that Italy has to offer – and that means some of the best food you will enjoy anywhere.

Primavera

SPRING

Spring

Spring is the opening of the food year. The new growth that sprouts now will mature in summer or autumn to be eaten then or stored for the winter. So I start my 'Four Seasons' in spring – the new beginning.

In Italy spring first arrives in Sicily in the far south. There is a natural abundance there, both on the land and in the sea – historically Sicily was the granary of Italy. After the heat of summer, the dryness of autumn and the bleak cold of winter, spring is when it all comes together with new moisture in the soil and warm days. The island literally blossoms as the almond and citrus trees come into flower and green shoots of young wheat cover the inland plains.

Remarkably this abundance happens in the sea as well, with the annual migration of tuna from the Atlantic to the warmer waters of the Mediterranean. For centuries the tuna catch has been one of the great events of the Sicilian calendar. Swordfish, another delicacy, also begin to appear off the east coast at this time.

Sicilian food has very strong regional characteristics. For centuries the island has absorbed influences from the great cultures of the Mediterranean, such as the Greeks, Carthaginians, Romans, Moors, Normans and Spanish.

The recipes I have chosen reflect both spring and the character of Sicilian cooking. Fish is a key ingredient (tuna, swordfish and sardines) and sheep's cheeses are excellent (particularly the famous soft ricotta). There are special pasta dishes (Sicilians claim dried pasta originated there) and lamb is a favourite for meat. To cap it off, Sicilians have a sweet tooth and produce an extraordinary range of cakes, pastries and ices for which they are justly famous.

Arancine

Savoury Rice Balls

Makes 15–20 arancine

300 g left-over risotto

1 large fresh mozzarella
  ball, cut into small cubes

2 thick slices cooked ham,
  very finely chopped

120 g unbleached plain flour

2 organic eggs, lightly
  beaten

200 g fresh breadcrumbs

500 ml sunflower oil,
  for frying

I love these little balls that are packed with flavour. You can eat them as a 'stuzzichino' – a taste-teaser before your meal – accompanied by a nice light red wine, or as part of an antipasto or even as a starter.

In Sicily they make these arancine bigger and pointy on one side. They are called 'arancine Mont Albano' after a well-known TV character, a detective who always stops his investigations for a good lunch or dinner.

Moisten your hands with a little water, then take a tablespoon of the risotto and flatten it gently in the palm of one hand. Place a cube of mozzarella and a little ham in the centre, then shape the risotto around the filling, forming it into a neat, tight ball. Add a little more risotto to cover the filling if necessary.

Roll the arancine in the flour, shaking off any excess. Dip them into the egg, then coat with breadcrumbs. Pat the arancine well with your hands to make sure they are nice and firm and evenly coated. Place them on a board, ready for frying.

Heat the oil in a medium saucepan. Deep-fry the arancine in batches over medium–high heat until golden, turning them frequently as they cook. Drain on kitchen paper and keep them warm while you cook the remainder. Serve immediately.

Variation

To make black squid ink arancine, use risotto made with fish stock – you could use left-over fish stock from Cus-cus di Pesce (page 58). Add a little squid ink to the risotto to make it black. Follow the same method as for the arancine recipe above, simply substituting prawns for the ham.

Fave con Pecorino

Broad Beans with Pecorino

Serves 4

400 g very young broad
  beans

200 g pecorino

60 ml good-quality virgin
  olive oil

sea salt flakes

I love to serve this very simple but delicious dish as a starter or even with pre-dinner drinks.

The best time to eat broad beans is when they are very young and tender. I first tried this wonderful combination of sweet, crunchy favas with the salty, strong flavour of the pecorino cheese in Tuscany. The farmer put a large basket of fresh fava beans on the table, cut a large chunk of pecorino cheese, produced with the milk from his own sheep, and poured some very fragrant new virgin olive oil. We all helped ourselves, shelling the beans, dipping them into the oil and eating them with a thin slice of cheese.

Pop the broad beans out of their pods. If they are very young there is no need to blanch and peel them.

Shave the pecorino over the beans and drizzle with olive oil. Sprinkle with salt and serve.

Giardiniera

Pickled Vegetables

**Makes 1 × 2 litre jar,
or 2 × 1 litre jars**

PICKLING LIQUID

800 ml good-quality
  white-wine vinegar

800 ml water

2 tablespoons honey

6 juniper berries

6 cloves

10 peppercorns

2–4 small red chillies

3 fresh bay leaves

8 very small pearl onions

4 small carrots, cut into
  4 cm sticks

4 celery stalks (the young,
  light-green ones), cut into
  4 cm sticks

½ small cauliflower, broken
  into small florets

200 g young green beans,
  tops and tails trimmed

10 cloves garlic, peeled

A jar of these fabulous tart and crunchy vegetables should be a part of every well-stocked pantry. They are eaten with pre-dinner drinks or as part of an antipasto.

I love them with Polpettone (page 319) or just some prosciutto.

Place all the pickling liquid ingredients into a large non-reactive saucepan. Bring to the boil, then cover the pan and simmer gently for 15 minutes.

Add the onions to the pan and simmer for 5 minutes. Add the remaining ingredients and, when the liquid returns to the boil, remove the pan from the heat.

Sterilise a 2 litre glass jar or 2 × 1 litre jars. Spoon the vegetables into the sterilised jar(s), and pour in enough of the pickling liquid to cover them completely. Seal and allow to cool. Refrigerate for 2 days before eating. Once opened, the giardiniera will keep for up to 2 months in the refrigerator.

Stuzzichino di Tonno

Tuna Starter

Serves 4–6

400 g canned tuna in oil, drained

50 g unsalted pistachio nuts, toasted and roughly chopped

25 g capers in brine, drained

6–8 cornichons (gherkins) in brine, drained and diced

125 ml good-quality virgin olive oil

This makes a delicious starter, or you can enjoy it as a snack during the day.

I first tried it on the island of Favignana on the western side of Sicily, a port town famous for the annual tuna catch – the 'matanza'. There you find the long, wide boats that have been used for centuries to net the tuna as they swim past on their seasonal migration.

Combine the tuna, pistachios, capers, and cornichons in a mixing bowl. Add the olive oil and use a fork to mix them together roughly – I prefer it to be a bit chunky.

Serve with crusty sourdough bread or lingue di suocera (page 107).

Sfincione

Pizza with Anchovies and Caciocavallo

Serves 4–6

PIZZA DOUGH

600 g unbleached plain flour, preferably Italian type 00

2 teaspoons salt

1 tablespoon dry yeast

3 tablespoons good-quality virgin olive oil

375–500 ml warm water

TOPPING

90–100 ml good-quality virgin olive oil

2 large Spanish onions, finely sliced

20 anchovy fillets in oil, drained and roughly broken up

20 black olives, pitted

200 g caciocavallo or pecorino, shaved

2 tablespoons fresh breadcrumbs

2 tablespoons fresh oregano, chopped

sea salt flakes and ground black pepper

To make the pizza dough, combine all the dough ingredients in a large mixing bowl. Turn the dough onto a work surface and knead until it becomes smooth, shiny and elastic. If it looks too dry, add a little more water. If it looks too wet, add a little more flour. Shape into a ball and rub with a little oil. Leave in a warm place, covered with a tea towel, for about an hour.

Preheat the oven to 220°C (gas mark 7).

Heat around 2 tablespoons of the oil in a large frying pan and add the onion. Fry for 5 minutes or until soft and translucent. Oil a 30 × 40 cm oven tray. Roll the pizza dough out and lift it onto the tray. Use your fingers to push the dough into the corners and to make indentations over the surface. Brush generously with olive oil. Spread the onion over the pizza base, followed by the anchovies, olives, cheese, breadcrumbs and oregano. Drizzle on the remaining oil and sprinkle with a few salt flakes and pepper. (Don't add too much salt as the anchovies and olives are already salty.)

Bake in the oven for about 20 minutes until golden-brown.

Insalata Pantesca

Potato and Tomato Salad

Serves 4

4 medium potatoes, boiled,
  peeled and sliced

1 small Spanish onion,
  very thinly sliced

8 ripe tomatoes, diced,
  or 16 cherry tomatoes

12 black or green olives,
  pitted

30 g capers in brine,
  drained and chopped

1 handful fresh basil leaves,
  chopped

1 handful fresh oregano
  leaves, chopped

80 ml good-quality virgin
  olive oil

salt and ground black
  pepper

I love this simple but delicious dish. It is perfect as a light lunch because it is so simple it does depend on the quality of the tomatoes.

When you buy tomatoes (or better still, pick them in your vegetable garden), make sure they are firm and fragrant. I don't put them in the fridge, as I find they lose a lot of flavour. Put them in a flat basket and leave them on the kitchen table. Of course the best way to have the most fragrant tomatoes is to grow your own. They are easy to grow and, together with herbs, are some of the most worthwhile ingredients to produce at home.

Gently combine the potato, onion, tomato, olives and capers in a large bowl.

Add the basil, oregano and oil, and toss together gently but thoroughly. Season and serve with plenty of crusty Italian bread.

Insalata di Polipini e Seppioline

Octopus and Calamari Salad

Serves 4

6 small octopus, about
   15 cm in length

6 small calamari

2 tablespoons good-quality
   red-wine vinegar

2 fresh bay leaves

finely grated zest and juice
   of 1 organic lemon

125 ml good-quality virgin
   olive oil

1 celery heart, sliced into
   1 cm pieces (including
   the small leaves)

sea salt flakes and ground
   black pepper

Clean the octopus by cutting off the head and eyes and removing the inside of the sack. Push the beak out through the legs and discard it.

Separate the tentacles from the calamari tubes. Slice the long body tubes open and remove the insides. Don't forget to pull out the long piece of clear cartilage from the tubes as well.

Place the vinegar and bay leaves in a large saucepan of water and bring it to the boil. Add the octopus and calamari (including tentacles) and boil for 10–15 minutes over medium heat. Remove the pan from the heat and leave the octopus and calamari to cool down in the water.

In a serving bowl, whisk together the lemon zest, juice and olive oil to form an emulsion. Stir in the celery.

Remove the octopus and calamari from the water and peel off the skin. Pull the legs apart and slice the bodies into thick strips. Pat everything dry on kitchen paper and add to the serving bowl. Season with salt flakes and pepper and toss everything together gently. I like to eat this salad at room temperature, as a starter.

Finissima di Tonno

Tuna Carpaccio

Serves 6

1 × 25 cm square sheet of
good-quality butter puff
pastry

sea salt flakes

200–300 ml sunflower oil,
for frying

6 teaspoons capers in brine,
drained

250–300 g sashimi-grade
tuna

good-quality virgin olive oil,
for drizzling

organic lemon juice,
for drizzling

1 small red chilli, very
finely sliced (optional)

The combination of the crisp saltiness of the fried capers and
the sweetness of the tuna is absolutely delicious.

You can serve these with pre-dinner drinks or as a light
first course.

Preheat the oven to 180°C (gas mark 4).

Cut the pastry sheet into 6 equal rectangles. Score the surface
on the diagonal with a sharp knife, and sprinkle with a few salt
flakes. Bake for 6 minutes, or until golden-brown.

Heat the sunflower oil in a small saucepan until hot. Fry the
capers until they turn crisp, then remove from the oil and drain
on kitchen paper.

Just before serving, arrange 3–4 slices of very thinly sliced
tuna on each pastry base. Drizzle over a little olive oil and lemon
juice, then sprinkle on the capers and chilli, if using. (There is
no need to season further as the capers are salty enough.)

Ricotta di Maria

Maria's Ricotta

Makes around 100 g

1 litre full-cream milk

1 teaspoon salt

80 ml white vinegar

180 ml water

Heat the milk (and salt, if using) in a large saucepan, stirring constantly. As soon as it boils, remove the pan from the heat.

Mix the vinegar and water together in a small jug. Pour it into the milk in a slow, steady stream, beginning in the centre then working out in a bigger and bigger circle until you reach the edge of the pan. You will see the milk start to separate.

Place the saucepan in a sink of very cold water. After a few minutes use a slotted spoon to lift the ricotta out and transfer it to a colander lined with a damp cheesecloth (muslin). Sit the colander on a plate and leave to drain. If you are not using it straight away, transfer it to the refrigerator.

The watery liquid that remains behind in the pan is called the whey. If it still looks a little cloudy and milky, return it to the boil. You will see it coagulate to form a little more ricotta. Put the pan back into the sink of cold water and lift the ricotta out with a slotted spoon and transfer to the colander.

The whey may be combined with more milk to make further batches of ricotta. I actually find the second, third and fourth batches are better, as they lose some of the acidity of the vinegar. If you don't plan to make more ricotta straight away, you can pour the whey into a glass jar and keep it in the refrigerator for up to 4 days.

Frittata

Italian Omelette

Serves 6

12 organic eggs

1 tablespoon water

salt and ground black
  pepper

4 heaped tablespoons
  grated parmigiano

2 large potatoes, boiled
  and chopped

1 Spanish onion or
  2 leeks, chopped

25 g unsalted butter

25 ml good-quality virgin
  olive oil

Frittatas are something I make very often, especially as part of
a lunch with other mixed dishes and salads – rather like a grand
antipasto.

They are easily prepared and look really appetising. You can
use your imagination and experiment with different vegetables.
I also find that the frittata tastes better when served cold.

Beat the eggs with a fork and add the water, salt, pepper,
parmigiano and chopped potatoes.

Fry the onion or leeks in the butter and oil until transparent
and add them and the chopped potatoes to the egg mixture. Put
a little oil or butter in a non-stick frying pan, pour in the egg
mixture and cook over medium heat for around 5 minutes. Then
turn the grill to medium and place the frittata under it. Grill for
about 5 minutes or until the frittata is golden-brown. Allow to
cool and slide onto a serving dish.

Variation

You can use all sorts of vegetables to make frittata, such as
asparagus, spinach or zucchini (courgettes), but lightly cook
the vegetables first.

Uova in Cocotte

Eggs in Cocotte

Serves 6

12 slices pancetta

4 tablespoons virgin olive oil

1½ large Spanish onions

120 g unsalted butter

600 g frozen chopped
    spinach, well-drained

salt and ground black
    pepper

12 large organic eggs

250 ml cream

150 g grated parmigiano

This is another dish that's very simple but full of flavour. Instead of spinach, you can experiment with other favourite vegetables.

I insist on organic eggs, not only because they are much healthier for you, but the flavour is so superior.

Preheat the oven to 200°C (gas mark 6).

Fry the pancetta in a small amount of oil in a frying pan until crisp, then let it drain on kitchen paper.

Chop the onions and fry them until soft in a little butter and oil. Add the spinach, salt and pepper and cook for a few minutes. Add the pancetta.

Butter 6 ramekins (you will need one medium ovenproof ramekin or bowl per person), and spread the spinach mixture evenly among the bowls. Make a small indentation in the spinach and gently break 2 whole eggs into each dish. Add about 2 tablespoons cream on top of the eggs, season with salt and pepper and scatter parmigiano over the top. Lastly, add a small knob of unsalted butter to each ramekin.

Bake in the oven for about 5–8 minutes. The egg yolks should still be soft when they are served.

Pasta alle Sarde

Pasta with Fresh Sardines

Serves 4–6

600 g fresh sardines

2 tablespoons salt

2 large bunches wild fennel

150 ml good-quality virgin
olive oil

1 large Spanish onion,
finely chopped

1 teaspoon ground cumin

1 teaspoon ground
cinnamon

1 teaspoon turmeric

1 teaspoon ground ginger

5 anchovy fillets in oil,
drained

50 g currants

50 g pine nuts, toasted

100 g fresh breadcrumbs

1 handful flat-leaf
parsley, chopped

1 handful mint, chopped

1 handful marjoram,
chopped

½ teaspoon saffron powder

salt and ground black
pepper

500 g strozzapreti or
bucatini pasta

Scrape away the scales from the sardines. Pull the heads away from the bodies – the backbones will naturally come away too. (Your fishmonger can do this for you if you prefer.) Dry the sardines well on kitchen paper.

Add the salt to a large saucepan of water and bring to the boil. Drop in the fennel and simmer for 5 minutes. Lift it out of the water and chop finely. Reserve the water for cooking the pasta.

To make the sauce, heat 3 tablespoons of the olive oil in a large frying pan. Add the onion and cook until soft and translucent. Stir in the spices and cook for a few more minutes. Add the anchovies, currants, pine nuts and half the sardines to the pan. Cook for around 5 minutes, stirring and breaking up the sardines with a fork.

Add the breadcrumbs, chopped fennel, herbs and saffron with another 2 tablespoons of olive oil. Season to taste and cook for a further 1–2 minutes.

Boil the pasta in the reserved fennel water until it is al dente.

Meanwhile, heat 2 tablespoons of the olive oil in a separate frying pan and quickly fry the remaining sardines until golden. Drain the pasta and tip half into a warm serving bowl. Stir in the rest of the olive oil and half of the sauce. Top with the remaining sauce and the fried sardines and toss together at the table.

Pasta alla Bottarga

Pasta with Sun-Dried Mullet Roe

Serves 4–6

500 g spaghetti

190 ml good-quality
virgin olive oil

10 anchovy fillets in
oil, drained

50 g fresh breadcrumbs

2 tablespoons baby capers
in brine, drained

½ bunch flat-leaf parsley,
chopped

½ bunch fresh mint,
chopped

20 cherry tomatoes, halved

100 g bottarga (sun-dried
mullet roe), membrane
removed, shaved or very
finely grated

salt and ground black
pepper

You can find bottarga at fish markets or good fish shops. The flavour is quite strong and salty, so it is used sparingly, rather as you would use salted anchovies. Try it very thinly sliced on a piece of buttered sourdough toast or on a bed of celery (page 129).

Boil the spaghetti in plenty of salted water.

While the pasta is cooking, heat 2 tablespoons of the olive oil in a small frying pan. Add the anchovies and stir them around in the oil until they melt. Add the breadcrumbs, capers, parsley and mint and toss over the heat for about 2 minutes, taking care not to burn the breadcrumbs. Remove the pan from the heat.

As soon as the pasta is cooked al dente, drain it, reserving about 125 ml of the cooking water.

Tip the pasta into a warm serving dish and stir in the reserved water. Stir in the remaining olive oil then add the breadcrumb mixture, tomatoes and bottarga. Toss everything together gently, then taste and adjust the seasoning to your liking. Serve immediately.

Pasta Primavera

Pasta with Spring Vegetables

Serves 4–6

50 g unsalted butter

3 baby leeks, trimmed
  and sliced

2 cloves garlic, crushed

1 small fennel bulb, very
  thinly sliced

1½ tablespoons salt

150 g podded baby broad
  beans, blanched
  and peeled

150 g baby green beans,
  cut into 3 cm lengths

150 g podded fresh peas

1 bunch thin asparagus,
  cut into 3 cm lengths

400 ml pure cream

500 g ditali pasta (small
  1 cm tubes)

salt and ground black
  pepper

100 g freshly grated
  parmigiano

This is a wonderful spring pasta dish. It relies on its impact from the new season's vegetables – the smaller the better. The flavour is delicate and fresh.

Melt the butter in a large frying pan. Add the leeks and cook gently for 5 minutes, then add the garlic and fennel and cook until soft.

Add the salt to a large saucepan of water and bring to the boil. When the water boils, drop in the broad beans, green beans, peas and asparagus. As soon as the water comes back to the boil, lift the vegetables out with a slotted spoon (reserve the water for cooking the pasta) and add them to the frying pan with the leek and fennel mixture. Pour in the cream and bring to the boil. Let it bubble for 2 minutes – the vegetables should still have a crunch – then remove the pan from the heat.

Boil the pasta in the vegetable water until al dente.

Drain the pasta well and add to the cream and vegetable mix. Toss everything together. Season with salt and pepper, add the parmigiano and serve immediately.

Pasta con Pesto alla Trapanese

Pasta with Pesto, Trapani-Style

Serves 4–6

PESTO

1 bunch fresh basil,
  leaves only

6 very ripe tomatoes,
  skin and seeds removed,
  roughly chopped

50 g fresh almonds

1–2 cloves garlic, crushed

50 g fresh breadcrumbs

125 ml good-quality virgin
  olive oil

salt and ground black
  pepper

500 g spaghettini or
  spaghetti

100 g dried salted ricotta or
  parmigiano, freshly grated

I first tried this pesto in Trapani, western Sicily. The almonds were still green outside so the kernels were soft and juicy. With the sweetness of the tomatoes it made a very special sauce.

You can also use this pesto on a bruschetta as a starter.

Put all the pesto ingredients into a mortar or food processor and blend to a coarse paste. Taste and adjust the seasoning to your liking.

Boil the pasta in plenty of salted water. As soon as the pasta is cooked al dente, drain it and tip it into a warm serving dish. Pour on the pesto and toss well. Take to the table straight away and serve with the ricotta or parmigiano on the side.

Ravioli di Michele

Michele's Ravioli

Serves 6

PASTA DOUGH

400 g semolina flour
(hard durum flour)

4 organic eggs

1–2 teaspoons salt

STUFFING

15 zucchini (courgette)
flowers (bitter stamens
removed), chopped

400 g fresh full-cream
ricotta

100 g freshly grated
parmigiano

1 handful fresh mint
leaves, finely chopped

salt and ground black
pepper

SAUCE

125 ml good-quality
virgin olive oil

125 ml water

15–20 zucchini (courgette)
flowers (bitter stamens
removed), finely sliced

1 handful fresh mint leaves,
finely sliced

150 g freshly grated
parmigiano

ground black pepper

For the dough, put the flour, eggs and salt into a food processor or electric mixer and mix with a dough hook until the pasta is smooth and elastic (about 5 minutes). Divide the dough into quarters and feed them through a pasta machine, working from the widest setting down to the second-finest setting. Sprinkle the pasta sheets with a little flour and set aside.

To make the stuffing, mix all the ingredients together then taste and adjust the seasoning to your liking. Be careful with the salt, though, as the cheese is already salty.

Use an 8 cm pastry cutter to cut out circles from the pasta dough. Place a heaped teaspoon of stuffing in the middle of each, then fold the dough in half over the stuffing and press firmly around the edges to seal.

Bring a large saucepan of salted water to the boil. Add the ravioli carefully and boil for 2 minutes until they float to the surface – they should still be al dente. Lift the ravioli out with a slotted spoon and transfer them to a warm serving dish.

To make the sauce, whisk the oil and water together to form an emulsion. Add the remaining ingredients then pour the sauce over the ravioli and serve immediately.

Torta Rustica alla Ricotta

Ricotta Pie

Serves 6

PASTRY

500 g unbleached plain flour

150 g unsalted butter,
  at room temperature

1 organic egg

125 ml medium–dry Marsala

50 g freshly grated pecorino

1 teaspoon salt

ground black pepper

FILLING

500 g fresh full-cream
  ricotta

150 g prosciutto,
  cut into strips

100 g freshly grated
  parmigiano

100 g pecorino piccante,
  grated

2 organic eggs

ground black pepper

This dish is fabulous for lunch, as an alternative to quiche.
Enjoy it with a crisp mixed green salad.

Put all the pastry ingredients into a food processor and pulse
until the dough is just amalgamated. Roll it into a ball and place
it in the refrigerator to rest for an hour.

Preheat the oven to 200°C (gas mark 6) and butter a 23 cm
ovenproof dish.

Break off just over half of the pastry and roll it out on a lightly
floured work surface to about 5 mm thick then lift it into the
prepared dish so the pastry comes up the sides.

Mix all the filling ingredients together and season with pepper.
(The cheeses and prosciutto are fairly salty, so don't add any salt.)
Pour the filling into the pastry and smooth the surface.

Roll out the remaining pastry and use it to cover the pie.
Press around the rim to seal the edges and prick the pie lid all
over with a fork. Transfer to the oven and bake for 30 minutes or
until golden-brown. Remove the pie from the oven and leave it to
cool down completely before serving. If it is still warm, the ricotta
will be too runny to cut into neat slices.

Sarde Beccafico

Stuffed Sardines, Beccafico Style

Serves 4

700 g fresh sardines

15 fresh bay leaves

1 handful each chopped
flat-leaf parsley and mint,
to serve

STUFFING

125–200 ml good-quality
virgin olive oil

5 anchovy fillets

100 g fresh breadcrumbs

2 tablespoons finely chopped
flat-leaf parsley

1 tablespoon capers in brine,
drained and finely chopped
(optional)

3 tablespoons currants

4 tablespoons pine nuts,
toasted

grated zest and juice of
1 organic lemon

1 teaspoon sugar

salt and ground black
pepper

Preheat the oven to 200°C (gas mark 6).

Scrape away the scales from the sardines. Pull the heads away from the bodies – the backbone will naturally come away too – making sure the tail stays attached to the two fillets. (Your fishmonger can do this for you.) Rinse them well then dry them on kitchen paper.

To make the stuffing, heat half the olive oil in a small frying pan, then add the anchovies and let them melt, stirring continuously for about a minute. Add the breadcrumbs and cook for another minute then add the parsley, mix well and take off the heat. Stir in the capers, currants, pine nuts, lemon zest (reserving the juice for later), sugar and a little salt and pepper.

Open out the sardines and lay them out flat on a work surface. Place a teaspoon of the stuffing mixture onto each fish, arranging it neatly along its length. Lift the sides of the fish up to enclose the stuffing and secure with 2 toothpicks.

Butter an ovenproof dish, around 18 × 30 cm. Arrange the stuffed sardines in the dish, packing them in tightly to prevent them from opening up. Tuck the bay leaves in between the sardines and sprinkle on any left-over stuffing mixture. Drizzle over the remaining oil and bake for 15 minutes until golden-brown.

Remove from the oven and pour on the reserved lemon juice. Add the fresh herbs just before serving. You can serve this dish hot or cold, although I like it best at room temperature.

Involtini di Pesce Spada ai Agrumi

Rolled Swordfish with Citrus

Serves 4

4 slices swordfish, around
  20 cm square × 5 mm thick

50 g fresh breadcrumbs

salt and ground black
  pepper

1 organic lemon, thinly
  sliced

1 handful fresh bay leaves

80 ml good-quality virgin
  olive oil

STUFFING

grated zest of 1 organic
  lemon

grated zest of 1 organic
  orange

2 fresh lemon or orange
  leaves (make sure they
  are young and tender)

80 g pecorino piccante,
  grated

1 small red chilli, deseeded
  (optional)

2 tablespoons good-quality
  virgin olive oil

30 g fresh breadcrumbs

This dish will bring the sunshine to your table. The combination of the lemon and orange zest with the heat of the chillies and the sharpness of the pecorino is quite extraordinary.

Swordfish is one of the joys of Sicilian cooking and this recipe comes from Salina. You can serve these little swordfish rolls hot or at room temperature.

Preheat the oven to 200°C (gas mark 6).

Use a sharp knife to cut the swordfish slices in half so you have 8 × 10 cm slices in total. Pat them dry on kitchen paper.

To make the stuffing, place all the ingredients into a food processor and pulse briefly to combine.

Lay the swordfish slices out on a work surface and top each with a teaspoon of the stuffing. Roll up and secure with a toothpick. Scatter the breadcrumbs out on your work surface and roll the involtini in the crumbs so they are evenly coated.

Butter an ovenproof dish. Arrange the involtini in the dish and season lightly with salt and pepper. Tuck lemon slices and bay leaves alternately in between the involtini, then drizzle on the oil. Bake for 10–15 minutes. Any left-over stuffing mixture can be sprinkled over the fish as you serve it.

Pesce Spada al Salmoriglio

Grilled Swordfish with Salmoriglio Sauce

Serves 4

SALMORIGLIO SAUCE

120 ml good-quality virgin
  olive oil

60 ml warm water

juice of 1 organic lemon

2 cloves garlic, very
  finely chopped

1 tablespoon finely chopped
  fresh oregano

1 tablespoon finely chopped
  flat-leaf parsley

1 small red chilli, partially
  deseeded and very finely
  chopped (optional)

4 × 150 g slices swordfish,
  about 1 cm thick

1 tablespoon good-quality
  virgin olive oil

salt flakes and ground
  black pepper

In Sicily swordfish, found in the waters off the island's long
coastline, is much appreciated. Perhaps this is because it has a
very delicate flavour, so even people who do not especially like
fish will love it. The salmoriglio sauce is a very traditional way
to prepare it.

Preheat the grill to high.

To prepare the sauce, whisk the oil in a mixing bowl and
very slowly add the warm water and lemon juice, whisking
continuously to form an emulsion. Add the garlic, herbs and
chilli (if using).

Pat the swordfish slices dry with kitchen paper and rub them
all over with oil. Grill for around 2 minutes on each side. Remove
the fish from the grill and season with salt and pepper. Serve
straight away, with the sauce spooned over the fish. Alternatively,
serve the sauce on the side in a warm jug.

Cus-cus di Pesce

Fish Couscous

Serves 6

FISH STOCK

1.5 kg assorted fish (use heads and bones for stock and reserve fish fillets for stew)

1 Spanish onion, quartered

4 celery stalks, roughly chopped

3 fresh bay leaves

2 teaspoons salt

FISH STEW

60 ml good-quality virgin olive oil

1 large Spanish onion, finely chopped

the heart from ½ bunch celery, finely chopped

3 cloves garlic, sliced

3 fresh bay leaves

400 g canned, crushed roma tomatoes

1 small red chilli, finely sliced

assorted fish fillets, cut into 5 cm chunks (see above)

1 blue swimmer crab

1.5 litres fish stock (see above)

salt and ground black pepper

½ teaspoon saffron powder

500 g good-quality couscous

In Sicily couscous is made by hand, mixing semolina flour with a little water and saffron. It is rolled between the fingers to form small grains, about half the size of peppercorns, which are left to dry on a wooden board. It is a lengthy process, so for this dish I have broken with tradition and suggested using good-quality purchased couscous.

For this recipe you can use various fish, such as blue eye, ling, sea bass, red mullet or grouper. Ask your fishmonger to clean and fillet the fish, and to keep all the heads and bones for you to use to make the stock.

To make the fish stock, put the fish heads and bones in a large saucepan and cover with cold water. Add the onion, celery, bay leaves and salt and bring to the boil. Simmer gently for 30 minutes, skimming off any scum that rises to the surface. Remove from the heat and strain through a fine sieve.

To make the stew, heat three-quarters of the olive oil in a large saucepan, add the onion, celery and garlic and fry gently for a few minutes until they soften. Add the bay leaves, tomatoes and chilli and simmer gently for about 15 minutes. Add the fish fillets to the pan, together with the crab. Cook for a few minutes then ladle in the fish stock, reserving 600 ml for the couscous, and simmer for 10–15 minutes. Taste, then season with salt and pepper.

Heat the reserved fish stock in a separate saucepan. Stir in the saffron powder then add the couscous. Add the remaining oil, stir well and leave to absorb (as per the packet instructions). Fluff the couscous up with a fork, adding a little more oil if need be. Tip the couscous out onto a warm serving plate and ladle on some of the fish stew. Serve the remaining fish stew on the side.

Involtini di Agnello con Asparagi

Rolled Lamb with Asparagus

Serves 6

800–900 g lamb backstraps (loins)

salt and ground black pepper

2 fresh fior di latte balls (cow's milk mozzarella)

24 anchovy fillets in oil, drained

2 bunches young asparagus

2 sprigs rosemary, stalks discarded

unbleached plain flour, for dusting

100 g unsalted butter

60 ml good-quality virgin olive oil

150 ml dry Marsala

Cut each lamb backstrap in half, then slice it lengthways into thirds (you will have 6 slices per backstrap). With a meat mallet, pound the lamb slices as thinly as you can into rectangles. Pat them dry on kitchen paper and season lightly to your liking (remember that the anchovies are salty).

Lay the lamb slices out on your work surface with the long edges facing you. Cut the mozzarella into very thin slices and place 1 slice on top of each piece of lamb – it should cover about a third of the lamb slice. Arrange 1 anchovy and 2 asparagus spears crossways on top of the cheese and sprinkle with a few rosemary leaves. Roll the lamb tightly around the filling and secure with a toothpick or string. Dust the involtini with flour, shaking off any excess.

In a large frying pan, fry the involtini in batches in the butter and oil with the rest of the rosemary. Turn them so they colour evenly. Transfer to a warmed dish.

Once the involtini are all cooked, add the Marsala and cook for a few minutes, scraping up any bits from the base of the pan. Return the involtini to the pan and roll them around in the sauce. Lower the heat and cover the pan. Cook gently for about 10 minutes, adding a little more Marsala or water if it seems too dry. Serve the involtini hot, straight from the pan.

Involtini con Carciofi

Rolled Veal with Artichokes

Serves 4

600 g veal backstraps (loins)

80 g prosciutto, finely diced

90 g unsalted butter
  at room temperature

juice of ½ organic lemon

2 artichokes

60 g unbleached plain flour

80 ml good-quality virgin
  olive oil

5 fresh sage leaves

150 ml dry white wine

salt and ground black
  pepper

Cut the veal into 8 thin slices and pat dry with kitchen paper. Mix the prosciutto into the softened butter.

Bring a saucepan of salted water to the boil, then add the lemon juice. Trim the artichoke stalks away and remove the tough outer leaves, then slice a third off the tops. Add them to the boiling water and cook for 2 minutes. Remove from the water and drain upside down on a rack. When cool enough to handle, cut each artichoke into 8 slices, removing hairy bits of choke as necessary.

Spread each slice of veal with a little of the butter mixture and top with 2 slices of artichoke. Roll the meat up tightly and secure with a toothpick or string.

Roll the involtini in the flour.

Heat the olive oil in a large frying pan then add the sage leaves and involtini. Turn them around in the oil so that they brown evenly all over. Add the wine and stir well, making sure you scrape up all the tasty bits from the bottom of the pan. Season with salt and pepper then cover the pan and simmer over a very low heat for 10–15 minutes. Add a little more wine if necessary. Serve hot.

Polpettine con Ricotta

Meatballs with Ricotta

Serves 6

800 g minced lamb

300 g fresh ricotta

50 g freshly grated
parmigiano

100 g unsalted butter

75 ml good-quality virgin
olive oil

1 large Spanish onion,
finely chopped

3 cloves garlic, crushed

2 teaspoons ground cumin

1 teaspoon ground
coriander

1 teaspoon ground
cinnamon

2 sprigs fresh rosemary,
stalks discarded and
leaves chopped

½ bunch flat-leaf parsley,
finely chopped

100 g pine nuts

60 g fresh breadcrumbs

2 organic eggs

salt and ground black
pepper

*The addition of ricotta makes the polpettine both a bit lighter and
more moist. The inclusion of the spices gives the mixture a little
unusual pep.*

Place the minced lamb, ricotta and parmigiano into a large
mixing bowl. Heat around 20 g of the butter and 2 tablespoons
of the oil in a frying pan. Add the onion and cook over a low heat
until it softens. Add the garlic, spices, herbs and pine nuts and
cook for another 5 minutes, stirring frequently. Remove the pan
from the heat and leave to cool.

Add the breadcrumbs and eggs to the lamb and cheeses. Tip
in the spicy onion mixture and season with salt and pepper. Use
your hands to mix everything together well. At this stage you
can cover the mince mixture and leave it in the refrigerator for
a few hours, or even overnight, until needed.

Roll spoonfuls of the mince into small balls between the palms
of your hands.

Fry the meatballs in batches using the remaining butter and
oil, turning on all sides until they are golden-brown. Transfer to
a serving dish and keep warm in the oven.

The meatballs are delicious served hot, warm or cold. If you
like, serve them with the Tomato Sauce from Timballo di Natalia,
(page 222).

Fritella

Young Broad Beans, Artichokes and Peas

Serves 4

3–4 artichokes

juice of 2 organic lemons,
  mixed with 1 litre water

75 ml good-quality virgin
  olive oil

50 g unsalted butter

20 shallots, finely sliced

400 g podded fresh broad
  beans, blanched and peeled

400 g podded fresh peas

salt and ground black
  pepper

½ bunch flat-leaf parsley,
  finely chopped

2 sprigs wild fennel,
  finely chopped

I love this vegetable dish. I think the sweetness of the artichokes combined with the broad beans and peas is a match made in heaven.

To prepare the artichokes, remove the tough outer leaves until they become pale in colour and tender. Slice a third off the tops. Cut them into quarters and remove the choke. Now slice the artichokes into thin wedges and quickly place them in the lemon water to prevent the flesh from discolouring.

Remove the artichokes from the lemon water and dry them thoroughly on kitchen paper. Heat 2 tablespoons of the oil and all the butter in a frying pan. Add the artichokes and shallots and cook gently for a few minutes.

Add 125 ml water to the pan. Stir in the broad beans and peas and cook until they are just tender, about 8 minutes. Season with salt and pepper and stir in the herbs and the remaining olive oil. Serve at room temperature.

Fondi di Carciofi con Spinaci

Artichoke Hearts with Spinach

Serves 4

50 g unsalted butter, plus extra knob

1 Spanish onion, chopped finely

3 garlic cloves, chopped finely

10 anchovies, chopped

1 chilli, chopped

800 g spinach, fresh or frozen

8 artichokes

juice of ½ organic lemon, mixed with 1 litre water

50 g dried breadcrumbs

good-quality virgin olive oil, for drizzling

salt and ground black pepper

Preheat the oven to 180°C (gas mark 4).

In a frying pan melt the butter and cook the onion and garlic until soft, then add the chopped anchovies and chilli. Squeeze all the water out of the spinach leaves and add them. Cook, stirring, for a few minutes.

Trim the artichoke stalks, leaving about 2 cm. Remove most of the leaves, leaving only the very tender, innermost ones. Cut the top two-thirds of the artichoke leaves off. Now, with your fingers, open the artichoke up, in order to expose the choke. With a sharp knife remove all the choke and put the cleaned artichokes one by one into the lemon water to prevent the flesh from discolouring.

Butter an ovenproof dish that the artichokes will fit into. Dry the artichokes well with kitchen paper, then spoon 2 heaped tablespoons of the spinach mix into each artichoke heart, pressing it down. Sprinkle some breadcrumbs over the artichokes, then a drizzle of virgin olive oil and a knob of butter. Season with salt and pepper.

Bake for 20–25 minutes. You can serve it immediately from the oven dish, but the artichokes are also nice eaten at room temperature.

Carciofi crudi con Parmigiano

Raw Artichokes with Parmigiano

Serves 4–6

3–4 artichokes

juice of 2 organic lemons,
  mixed with 1 litre water

125 ml good-quality virgin
  olive oil

sea salt flakes and ground
  black pepper

thin shavings of fresh
  parmigiano, for serving

If you can find the small reddish artichokes with a spike at the end of the leaves, they are the best for this salad. The leaves are more tender than the green variety and they have no choke to remove. Unfortunately the season for these artichokes is very short. If you can't find this variety, use small early-season green ones.

Cut the top half of the artichokes away crossways, then cut the stem part in half lengthways. Put the pieces in the lemon water to prevent the flesh from discolouring.

Mix the remaining lemon juice, olive oil, salt and pepper and put this into a serving dish.

If the artichokes have a choke, cut it out very carefully and then slice them very finely. Dry the slices on kitchen paper. Immediately put the artichoke slices in the lemon and olive oil sauce. Add the parmigiano slices to the artichokes, and serve.

Asparagi con Burro Fuso e Parmigiano

Asparagus with Melted Butter and Parmigiano

Serves 4

3 bunches asparagus

150 g freshly grated
parmigiano

100 g unsalted butter

sea salt and ground black
pepper

When asparagus is in season this is my favourite lunch. I like the very thin green asparagus and I eat it with fried eggs.

Cook the asparagus in an asparagus pan if you have one, or steam them. Do not overcook – make sure the stalks are still a little crunchy. Drain the asparagus and arrange on a heated serving dish.

Sprinkle the parmigiano on the tips of the asparagus. Melt the butter and, as soon as it is foaming, pour it over the parmigiano. (The heat of the butter will melt the cheese and make a delicious crust.) Add a little salt and pepper. Serve at once with some crunchy Italian ciabatta bread.

Variation

For a more substantial meal you can fry 2 organic eggs per person and serve them on the plate with the asparagus. Make sure the yolks are still very runny.

Cassata Siciliana

Sicilian Cassata

Serves 6

MARIA'S SPONGE CAKE

butter, for greasing

3 organic eggs

125 g caster sugar

150 g self-raising flour

1 teaspoon baking powder

pinch of salt

grated zest of 1 organic
  lemon

2 tablespoons hot water

RICOTTA FILLING

800 g fresh ricotta

300 g caster sugar

3 tablespoons Marsala

100 g dark chocolate,
  chopped into little pieces

100 g candied fruit
  (optional)

MARZIPAN

200 g ground almonds

200 g icing sugar

2 teaspoons orange-blossom
  water or rosewater

1 drop green food colouring

around 50 ml water

GARNISH

candied fruit (optional)

melted dark or white
  chocolate (optional)

There is a saying in Sicily if a girl is very beautiful that she is 'bella come una cassata' (as beautiful as a cassata). As they love beautiful girls you can imagine how much they like their cassata.

Preheat the oven to 180°C (gas mark 4).

Line a 30 × 20 cm rectangular cake tin with greaseproof paper then butter the paper generously.

To make the sponge, beat the eggs until light and fluffy then, still beating, gradually add the sugar. Slowly mix in the flour, baking powder, salt and lemon zest, followed by the water. Pour the mixture into the prepared cake tin. Cook for about 8 minutes, or until firm to the touch.

Remove from the oven and leave to cool in the tin for a few minutes before turning out onto a cake rack. When cold, carefully cut the sponge horizontally through the centre, creating 2 thin slices. Then cut out 2 × 21 cm circles and cut the rest of the sponge into wide strips.

Line the base and side of a 22 cm springform cake tin with greaseproof paper. Arrange one sponge circle in the bottom of the cake tin and neatly line the side with the strips of cake so there are no gaps.

To make the ricotta filling, beat the ricotta with the sugar and Marsala until smooth. Fold in the chocolate and candied fruit, if using. Spoon the filling into the sponge-lined cake tin. Place the remaining sponge circle on top and press gently. Cover and transfer to the refrigerator for a few hours or, better still, overnight.

To make the marzipan, combine the ground almonds, icing sugar, flower water and food colouring with just enough water to form a stiff paste. Roll out the marzipan to 1 cm thickness. Turn the cassata out onto a serving plate and cover with marzipan. Decorate with more candied fruit or patterns in melted chocolate, if desired.

Crostata alla Marmellata di Arance

Orange Marmalade Tart

Serves 6

250 g good-quality bitter
  marmalade (home-made
  is best)

PASTRY

200 g unbleached plain flour

100 g unsalted butter,
  at room temperature

3 organic egg yolks

50 g caster sugar

pinch of salt

grated zest of 1 organic
  lemon

This tart is very special. The thin, crunchy base marries so well
with the bitter-sweetness of the marmalade.

Put all the pastry ingredients into a food processor and pulse in
quick bursts. When the dough is well amalgamated, roll it into
a ball and place it in the refrigerator to rest for 30 minutes.

Preheat the oven to 200°C (gas mark 6) and generously butter
a 23 cm pie dish or a springform tin.

Roll the pastry out on a lightly floured work surface, reserving
a little pastry for the decoration. Lift the pastry onto the buttered
pie dish and gently press into the dish. Roughly trim the edges
to fit.

Spread the marmalade over the base. Use the remaining pastry
to cut out little decorations and arrange them on the marmalade.

Bake on the bottom shelf of the oven for 20–25 minutes. Leave
to cool in the pie dish completely before carefully sliding out onto
a serving dish.

Crostata al Amaretto e Cioccolato

Amaretti and Chocolate Tart

Serves 6

PASTRY

250 g self-raising flour

120 g caster sugar

2 organic egg yolks

120 g unsalted butter,
at room temperature

pinch of salt

FILLING

4 organic egg whites

75 g bitter chocolate, finely
chopped

75 g almonds, toasted and
finely chopped

75 g amaretti biscuits,
finely chopped

icing sugar, for dusting

Put all the pastry ingredients in a food processor and pulse until the dough is just amalgamated. Roll it into a ball and place it in the refrigerator to rest for an hour.

Preheat the oven to 180°C (gas mark 4) and butter a 23 cm springform cake tin.

Roll the pastry out on a lightly floured work surface then lift it into the prepared tin so the pastry comes up the sides.

To make the filling, beat the egg whites until they form stiff peaks, but are not dry. Fold in the chocolate, almonds and amaretti. Pour the filling into the pastry shell and bake for around 35 minutes.

Remove the tin from the oven. Release the sides of the tin and remove the tart. Leave it to cool completely and serve dusted with icing sugar.

Torta Ornella

Ricotta, Almond and Lemon Cake

Serves 6–8

250 g unsalted butter,
  at room temperature

250 g caster sugar

6 organic eggs, separated

250 g almonds, roasted
  then ground

75 g self-raising flour

pinch of salt

finely grated zest of
  5 organic lemons and
  juice of 4 organic lemons

400 g fresh ricotta

I love this light, moist cake which combines some of the famous flavours of Sicily.

Ornella is a cheesemaker from the hills outside Modica in southeastern Sicily. When she made it for me the ricotta was so fresh it was still warm.

Preheat the oven to 180°C (gas mark 4).

Butter a 25 cm round springform cake tin. Beat the butter and sugar in an electric mixer until very light and fluffy. With the motor running, add the egg yolks, one at a time, until all are incorporated.

Combine the ground almonds with the flour, salt and lemon zest. Fold into the batter.

Whisk the lemon juice with the ricotta until light and airy. Fold into the cake batter.

Beat the egg whites until they form soft peaks. Fold them carefully into the batter.

Pour the batter into the prepared cake tin and bake for 50 minutes. Test for doneness by inserting a skewer into the cake. It should come out clean when cooked through.

Remove the cake from the oven and turn it out onto a cake rack to cool. It will remain nice and moist for a few days. Traditionally this delicious dessert or afternoon tea cake is served with a glass of Marsala.

Impanatigghi

Biscuits from Modica

Makes around 20 biscuits

PASTRY

300 g unbleached plain flour

150 g unsalted butter,
  at room temperature

80 g caster sugar

1 organic egg, plus
  1 organic egg yolk

¼ teaspoon salt

grated zest of 1 organic
  lemon

FILLING

250 g ground almonds

150 g caster sugar

grated zest of 1 organic
  lemon

2 teaspoons ground
  cinnamon

50 g finely minced lean beef

100 g dark chocolate, melted

few drops of good-quality
  Marsala, to moisten
  if necessary

Place all the pastry ingredients in a food processor and pulse until the dough amalgamates. Roll into a ball, cover in plastic wrap and refrigerate for 30 minutes.

Preheat the oven to 180°C (gas mark 4).

To make the filling, mix all the ingredients together well to form a thickish paste. If it seems too dry, add a few drops of Marsala.

Roll the pastry out as thinly as you can on a lightly floured work surface. With a pastry cutter, cut out circles of around 6 cm. With a sharp knife make a small 1 cm incision along the bottom third of each circle.

Spoon the filling into a piping bag and pipe around 3 cm of filling widthways across the centre of each pastry circle, parallel with the incision. Brush the rim with a little water, then fold the pastry over to create a half moon. Make sure the little cut is uppermost. Press around the rim to seal and trim away any excess pastry.

Line an oven tray with greaseproof paper. Lift the filled biscuits onto the tray and bake for 15–20 minutes until golden-brown. Remove from the oven and transfer to a rack to cool. They will keep in an airtight jar for about a week.

Semifreddo al Zabaglione

Marsala Ice Cream

Serves 8

6 organic eggs, separated

110 g caster sugar

150 ml good-quality Marsala

500 ml full cream, whipped

This is a sophisticated dessert, something of a classic.

Marsala, from the south-west of Sicily, is a sweet fortified wine that gives the ice cream a velvety texture.

Beat the egg yolks and sugar together until light, then add the Marsala and beat again until light and fluffy.

Place the bowl over a double boiler, allow the water in the lower pan to simmer, and whisk the mixture until it increases in volume and becomes like a thick cream. Set aside and allow it to cool.

Beat the egg whites until stiff but not dry. Mix the whipped cream with the egg yolk, sugar and Marsala mixture, then fold in the egg whites. Pour into a 30 × 30 cm square dish, cover with plastic wrap and put in freezer for at least 6 hours.

Scoop the ice cream out and put it into glasses to serve. The ice cream should still be a little bit soft – 'semifreddo' means 'half-frozen'.

Sorbetto al Cioccolato

Chocolate Sorbet

Serves 6

1 litre water

250 g caster sugar

200 g cocoa powder,
  preferably a good-quality
  Swiss or Belgian variety

1 tablespoon ground coffee

½ cup crème de cacao
  (optional, see Variation)

250 ml thick (double)
  cream (optional)

Chocolate is usually used to flavour ice cream rather than sorbet, but this unusual sorbet has very a strong chocolate taste. It is delicious on its own or served with slightly runny fresh cream on the top that hardens on contact with the sorbet to form a snowcap on the chocolate. To be successful it requires a very good-quality bitter cocoa powder, ideally Swiss or Belgian.

Bring the water to the boil and dissolve the sugar in it. Put the cocoa powder and ground coffee into a bowl, add a little of the hot syrup and mix to a thick paste. Then add the rest of the water. Taste for sweetness and adjust if necessary by adding more sugar. Allow to cool, put into an ice cream maker and churn.

This sorbet is delicious served with some lightly whipped thick cream.

Variation
You can add the crème de cacao to the sorbet before it is frozen, or pour it over later – or both if you prefer!

Cannoli

Ricotta-filled Sweet Pastry Rolls

Makes around 12 cannoli

PASTRY

25 g unsalted butter,
   at room temperature
   (traditionally lard is used
   instead of butter in this
   recipe)

150 g self-raising flour

1 organic egg, separated

1 tablespoon caster sugar

80 ml dry Marsala

pinch of salt

2 tablespoons bitter
   cocoa powder

FILLING

250 g fresh ricotta

125 g icing sugar

30 g good-quality dark
   chocolate (70% cocoa
   solids), chopped into
   small chunks

finely grated zest of
   1 organic lemon

finely grated zest of
   1 organic orange

sunflower oil, for frying

icing sugar, for dusting

Put all the pastry ingredients into a food processor and pulse to form a dough. It will be smooth and firm, similar to pasta dough. Form it into a ball and let it rest, covered with a cloth, for about 1 hour.

While the dough is resting, make the ricotta filling. Whisk the ricotta with the sugar until it is light and fluffy. Mix in the chocolate and both citrus zests, then refrigerate until needed.

Roll the pastry out to about 3 mm thick (I find it easiest to feed it through a pasta machine). Cut the pastry into 8 cm squares and lay them out on a floured work surface.

Brush metal cannoli cylinders lightly with oil. Wrap a piece of pastry on the diagonal around each cylinder. Use the egg white left over from making the pastry to moisten the edges where they overlap, and press them together gently to seal.

Pour the sunflower oil into a medium-sized saucepan to a depth of around 6 cm. When the oil is hot, fry the cannoli in batches of 3 until golden-brown. Drain well on kitchen paper and slide them off the metal cylinders while still warm.

When the cannoli are completely cold, spoon the ricotta filling into a piping bag and fill the cannoli shells generously. Dust with icing sugar and serve. They are best eaten on the day they are made.

LM 208 D

Estate

SUMMER

Summer

I have always thought Italian food was suited to summer. The style is casual and direct, prepared in an unpretentious way so it lets the fresh ingredients speak for themselves.

For nearly everyone in Italy, summer means dreams of the sea. With its long coastline and numerous islands, Italy presents no shortage of opportunities for a beach holiday. Therefore, as you would expect, there is a huge range of seafood dishes available. There are also the wonderful summer vegetables – tomatoes, capsicums (peppers), zucchini (courgettes), cucumbers, fennel, eggplants (aubergines) and celery. These, rather than leaf vegetables, form the basis of traditional summer salad dishes in Italy.

As a family we used to go to a house in Sardinia for our summer holidays so a number of the recipes I have chosen have a Sardinian accent. Sicily also gets a look in with the classic Caponatina and Involtini di Melanzane. I also first tasted Granita al Gelso on the island of Salina off Sicily.

There are pizzas of course. The pizza started off as street food in Naples (which is still probably the best place to eat pizza) before it found worldwide fame. It's ideal as a casual meal in summer.

There is very little meat. However, the classic Vitello Tonnato has to be included and the very festive Pollo Capriccioso. As a surprise, there is a Persian rice and lamb recipe (we always had it in summer so I had to include it) which my mother learnt when we lived in Iran in the 1950s.

Occasionally at the seaside you need a great festive dish. Pesce al Sale – fish covered in salt and baked – looks spectacular as it arrives at the table for the salt crust to be crushed to release its tantalising aromas.

# Mandorle

Spiced Almonds

Serves 4

2 tablespoons good-quality
virgin olive oil

2 cloves garlic, thinly sliced

6–8 fresh sage leaves

1–2 sprigs fresh rosemary

250 g whole almonds,
skinless if desired

1 chilli, finely chopped
(optional, if you like it hot)

sea salt flakes

Italians love their 'aperitivi', the traditional pre-dinner drinks, wine or special vermouths, eaten with savoury nibbles called 'stuzzichini'.

In Sardinia we used to go down to a bar on the marina at Porto Cervo and have Campari with fresh orange juice and these wonderful, tasty almonds.

I grow sage and rosemary in my garden. They are two herbs that are really rewarding when used fresh in cooking. I find their flavour more intense and the variety of dishes you can use them in is endless. If space is an issue, they grow very well also in pots.

In a small saucepan, heat the olive oil over medium heat. Add the garlic, sage leaves and rosemary.

Place the almonds and chilli, if using, into the pan and fry them until they start to brown.

Pour off any extra olive oil, add the sea salt flakes and serve.

Variation
You can use other nuts instead of almonds, such as hazelnuts, pecans or cashews.

Tapanata

Tapenade

Serves 4

500 g good-quality black
  or green olives, pitted

2 cloves garlic

100 g anchovy fillets

50 g capers

1 chilli

a few leaves fresh basil

400 ml good-quality virgin
  olive oil

salt and ground black
  pepper

toasted bread or crackers,
  to serve

I often make this tapanata. When made with green olives rather than black, it tastes quite different. Black ones are the ripe olives, so they have a softer and rounder taste. Green ones, not so ripe and harder, have a little more bite to them. It's a matter of taste, so try both and see which you prefer.

Place the olives, garlic, anchovy fillets, capers, chilli and basil in a food processor and blend, adding the oil slowly in a fine stream until you have the desired consistency.

Taste and season with salt and pepper. Serve with crunchy bread or crackers.

Note
The tapanata keeps very well in the fridge for at least one week. Just pour it into a clean jar, bang the jar on the table to make sure there are no air pockets and seal the tapanata with a thin layer of virgin olive oil.

Pâté di Anguilla

Smoked Eel Pâté

Serves 4

1 whole smoked eel,
  about 500 g

125 g unsalted butter,
  at room temperature

juice of 1 organic lemon

⅓ red onion, finely sliced

salt and ground black
  pepper

Eel is one of those rather unloved fish. I suppose it looks a bit unattractive (but how beautiful is octopus?). I think it's more that we usually do not know what to do with it.

This is a delicious way to prepare eel. It has a rich, rather fatty flesh that is perfect for pâté. Smoking enhances the flavour and the lemon juice adds a delicious sharpness. This is one of the great fish pâtés.

Skin the eel and remove the backbone. Place the flesh, broken into pieces, in a food processor with the butter, lemon juice and onion. Process until it becomes a smooth mousse. Taste and season with salt and pepper, then refrigerate until needed.

Note
You can buy eel at fish markets. It is usually sold vacuum-packed.

Salsa Verde

Parsley, Coriander and Dill Sauce

Serves 4–6

1 small bunch flat-leaf
  parsley

½ bunch coriander

½ bunch dill

1 teaspoon Dijon mustard

juice of 1 organic lemon

1 chilli (optional)

1 organic egg yolk

250 ml good-quality virgin
  olive oil

salt and ground black
  pepper

Place all the ingredients, except the oil and seasoning, in a food processor, and mix very well. Then add the oil very slowly, in a fine stream, as if you were making mayonnaise. The salsa verde should be quite thick in consistency. Add salt and pepper to taste.

Variations

The herbs that go into a salsa verde (green sauce) can be a matter of taste. To accompany lamb, use flat-leaf parsley and mint.
For grilled vegetables, you could use flat-leaf parsley and basil.

Note

If you want to keep it for a few days, pour it into a jar, bang the jar on the table to make sure there are no air pockets in the sauce and then pour a thin layer of virgin olive oil over it. Keep in the refrigerator for up to one week.

Acciugata

Anchovy Dip

Serves 6

300 g anchovies

500 ml good-quality virgin
olive oil

6 cloves garlic

2 teaspoons chopped fresh
thyme

3 teaspoons chopped fresh
basil

3 teaspoons Dijon mustard

3 teaspoons red wine
vinegar

1 chilli

ground black pepper

assorted raw vegetables,
such as carrot, celery,
red and yellow capsicums
(peppers), Lebanese
cucumber, and radishes

You can use this as part of a mixed antipasto or as a light
first course.

Place the anchovies, olive oil, garlic, thyme, basil, mustard,
red-wine vinegar and chilli in a food processor. Blend until
you have a finely textured sauce. Season with pepper to taste.

Cut the vegetables into long strips and arrange on a plate.
Serve the sauce seperately, so that you can dip the vegetables
into it.

Note

I prefer to use anchovies in oil for this dish, as they are less salty
than the salt-preserved ones. Just make sure you buy very good
quality ones.

Impasto per Pizza

Pizza Dough

Makes 4 pizzas, approximately 30 × 40 cm each

1 kg unbleached plain flour, preferably Italian type 00

15 g salt

15 g dry yeast

2 tablespoons good-quality virgin olive oil, plus extra for drizzling

625–750 ml warm water

With this basic pizza dough recipe you can also make grissini (thin bread sticks) or lingue di suocera (mother-in-law's tongues), which are very thin crisp-breads.

Mix together the dry ingredients with the oil and enough water to form a dough. Knead until the dough becomes shiny and elastic. Shape into a ball, place in a bowl and sprinkle a few drops of oil over the dough so that it does not dry out. Cover with a cloth and let stand in a warm spot for about 1 hour.

Punch the dough down, knead again well and, if you have time, let it rise again.

Note

If you like, once you have kneaded the pizza dough, you can put it in a bowl, cover it with cling film and put it in the fridge overnight. The next day let the dough come to room temperature, then proceed in making your pizza or breads.

Pizza Bianca

White Pizza

**Makes 4 pizzas,
approximately 30 × 40 cm
each**

1 quantity pizza dough
  (page 107)

2–3 leeks, finely chopped

25 g unsalted butter

25 ml good-quality virgin
  olive oil, plus extra for
  drizzling

2–3 medium potatoes,
  sliced paper-thin

sea salt flakes

ground black pepper

a few sprigs fresh rosemary,
  stems discarded

Not all pizzas have a topping of tomatoes and cheese. In fact, the original street-food pizzas in Naples (from where the pizza comes) had neither. This is a rather refined pizza, very tasty and visually appealing, that makes a delicious change from the classic.

Preheat the oven to 240°C (gas mark 9). Make the pizza dough on page 107.

Cook the leeks in a pan in a little butter and olive oil for about 10 minutes, until soft and sweet. Take a piece of dough (about 150–200 g), flatten it until it is about 1 cm thick and place it on an oiled oven tray. Spread the cooked leeks evenly over the dough and then arrange the potatoes like fish scales all over the pizza.

Sprinkle some salt and pepper on top, then drizzle olive oil all over the pizza, with some rosemary. Cook in the oven for about 10–15 minutes or until the base is golden-brown and crunchy.

Tip

If you have a pizza oven, the pizza will only take 5 minutes to cook, so you should boil the potatoes until tender beforehand, then slice them and put them on the dough, otherwise they will be too raw.

Pizza Margherita

Pizza Margherita

Makes 4 pizzas,
approximately
30 × 40 cm each

1 quantity pizza dough
  (page 107)

2 cloves garlic, crushed

1 × 400 g can peeled
  roma tomatoes

1 fresh large mozzarella
  or 6 mozzarella Ovolini

6–8 fresh basil leaves

salt and ground black
  pepper

good-quality virgin olive oil,
  for drizzling

This is the classic 'modern' pizza. In an inspired piece of 19th-century marketing (we are talking 150 years ago) it was named after an Italian princess, the Principessa Margherita, who would become the first queen of a united Italy.

The red, white and green of the tomato, mozzarella and basil represented the flag colours of the new Italy. So, if you like, it was a political pizza, as well as being so delicious, and it has taken the world by storm.

Preheat the oven to 240°C (gas mark 9).

Roll out the dough onto an oiled oven tray – the dough should be about 5 mm thick. Spread the garlic over the dough.

Drain the tomatoes of their juice and seeds and chop roughly. Spread the tomato over the dough. Break the mozzarella into little pieces and spread evenly on top of the tomato. Tear the basil leaves and sprinkle over the pizza and season. Lastly, sprinkle some olive oil over the whole pizza.

Cook in the oven for about 10–15 minutes, or in a pizza oven for 3–5 minutes, until the base is golden and crunchy.

Pizza al Prosciutto e Ruggola

Prosciutto and Rocket Pizza

Makes 4 pizzas, approximately
30 × 40 cm each

1 quantity pizza dough
(page 107)

1 × 400 g can peeled
roma tomatoes

150 g tomato paste
(optional)

1–2 cloves garlic, crushed

1 chilli, finely sliced

100 g prosciutto,
in long slices

good-quality virgin olive oil,
for drizzling

50 g piece of parmigiano

1 bunch rocket leaves,
roughly chopped

sea salt flakes and ground
black pepper

Preheat the oven to 240°C (gas mark 9).

Roll out the dough onto an oiled oven tray – the dough should be about 5 mm thick.

Drain the tomatoes of all their liquid. Chop them roughly and drain again – the tomatoes should not be wet. (You can add the tomato paste if you prefer a stronger flavour.)

Spread the garlic and chilli evenly over the pizza base, add the tomatoes and then some prosciutto. Drizzle a little olive oil over.

Cook in the oven for about 5–10 minutes, or in a pizza oven for about 3–5 minutes, until the bottom of the base is golden.

Remove from the oven. With a potato peeler, shave some parmigiano over the pizza and top with the rocket. Then drizzle some more olive oil over the pizza and season.

Ricotta al Forno

Baked Ricotta

Serves 4

500 g ricotta

2 organic eggs

100 g parmigiano

a few fresh oregano leaves

1 chilli, deseeded and
  finely sliced

salt and ground black
  pepper

This is a really delicious way to prepare ricotta. It looks very inviting and can be served on its own or as part of an antipasto.

It keeps well for a few days in the fridge.

Preheat the oven to 200°C (gas mark 6).

Mix all the ingredients together well in a bowl. Butter an ovenproof dish, place the mixture in the dish and bake for about 25 minutes until golden and puffed up.

You can eat this dish hot, but it has more flavour when cold.

Note

You can buy fresh ricotta at your deli or supermarket. Make sure you buy the full-cream milk ricotta and not the fat-reduced version.

Nudi

Ricotta and Spinach Gnocchi

Serves 8

1.25 kg frozen whole baby spinach (not chopped), thawed

500 g ricotta

2 organic egg yolks and 2 whole organic eggs, beaten together

150 g grated parmigiano, plus extra 100 g for the table

salt and ground black pepper

plain flour, for dusting

100 g unsalted butter

a few fresh sage leaves

'Nudi' in Italian means 'naked'. They are called this because they are essentially a ravioli filling but without the pasta.

Squeeze all the water out of the spinach (this is very important) and chop it roughly. With a fork thoroughly whisk the ricotta, eggs, 150 g parmigiano, salt and pepper, then mix in the spinach. Take about 1 tablespoon of this mixture at a time and roll it into little balls, dusting with flour.

Boil some salted water, turn the heat down and drop about 5 balls at a time into the water. As soon as they float to the surface, they are ready (about 1 minute). With a small sieve, fish them out and put them on a heated serving dish, in a single layer. Sprinkle a generous amount of parmigiano over the nudi.

Melt the butter with the sage. When it foams, pour it over the nudi and serve immediately.

Gnocchi alla Romana

Roman Gnocchi

Serves 4

1 litre milk

500 ml water

1–2 teaspoons salt

250 g coarse semolina

2 organic egg yolks

ground black pepper

150 g grated parmigiano

2–3 tablespoons fresh
  breadcrumbs

100 g butter

a few fresh sage leaves
  (optional)

Place the milk and water in a large pan, add the salt and bring to the boil. Add the semolina slowly, in a very fine and constant stream, whisking continuously with a whisk so as not to form lumps. Cook for about 10 minutes, stirring constantly with a wooden spoon. Then allow the semolina to cool slightly.

Stir in the egg yolks, pepper and about half the parmigiano, then taste for salt and add more if necessary.

Place some greaseproof paper on your kitchen bench and pour the semolina onto the paper, flattening it with the blade of a knife to about 1 cm thickness. Allow it to cool completely.

Preheat the oven to 200°C (gas mark 6).

Butter an ovenproof dish, about 5–6 cm deep. With a biscuit cutter or a glass of about 3 cm diameter, cut out little discs of the semolina mixture then arrange them in the dish with the discs overlapping slightly, like fish scales.

Sprinkle the breadcrumbs and the remaining parmigiano on top of the semolina discs. Cut the butter into little cubes and place on top of the gnocchi and, finally, add the sage leaves, if using. Bake in the oven for about 20 minutes, or until golden-brown.

Variations

To this basic recipe, you can add about 400 g finely chopped spinach to the milk, for green gnocchi. Alternatively, add about 300 g mashed baked pumpkin – these gnocchi will be softer than the basic recipe, therefore a little more difficult to handle, but the sweetness of the pumpkin is absolutely delicious.

Risotto di Pasta

Pasta Risotto

Serves 4

1 large Spanish onion

25 ml good-quality virgin
  olive oil

25 g unsalted butter

500 g small pasta shells

200 ml dry white wine

2 litres fresh, strong
  chicken stock

2 tablespoons freshly grated
  parmigiano, plus extra
  for serving

This dish was created by my grandfather, Ettore Biaggi, who was
a well-known restaurateur and chef in Lugano. During the war
the border with Italy was closed and it was difficult to buy rice in
Switzerland. He loved risotto, so his idea was to try pasta instead.
He used shell-shaped pasta as each piece contained a little of the
delicious risotto broth. It became a big hit in his restaurant.

Chop the onion and sauté in a pan with the olive oil and half the
butter until it has softened.

Add the pasta shells and cook for 1–2 minutes, stirring
well. Add the wine and let it evaporate.

Add half the stock, bring to the boil and cook, stirring
occasionally. If it gets too dry, add more stock. The pasta should
still be al dente when ready – about 8–10 minutes.

Remove from the stove, add the remaining butter and
parmigiano and stir well. (The pasta should be quite moist.)

Serve immediately with extra parmigiano.

Culligiones

Sardinian Ravioli

Serves 6 (makes about 24 large ravioli)

PASTA

450 g unbleached plain flour, preferably Italian type 00

4 organic eggs

1 tablespoon good-quality virgin olive oil

salt

extra flour, for dusting

FILLING

2 leeks, finely chopped

1 clove garlic, chopped

25 g unsalted butter

25 ml good-quality virgin olive oil

500 g boiled and mashed potatoes

5–6 mint leaves (this is the original way, but I prefer fresh sage leaves instead)

100 g grated parmigiano, plus extra for serving

60 g Sardinian pecorino

salt and ground black pepper

BURNT SAGE BUTTER

100–150 g unsalted butter

15 fresh sage leaves

This is a traditional pasta dish from the island of Sardinia.

We used to go to a restaurant located in a magic position high above the sea, nestled into the granite rocks. The chef, Gennaro, used wild mint from the island. The flavour is closer to that of sage than our mint, which is why I prefer sage for this dish.

For the filling, gently fry the leek and garlic together in the butter and oil until they are soft and the leeks are sweet. Then mix with all the remaining filling ingredients.

For the pasta, mix the flour, eggs, oil and salt in a food processor, using a dough hook, until you get a shiny ball of dough. Divide into 4 or 5 pieces and roll these into strips using a pasta machine, starting at the thickest setting and rolling them five times, folding the sheets into three each time before you re-roll. Gradually reduce to the second-finest setting.

Lay a pasta sheet on a surface dusted with flour. Place tablespoons of filling on the pasta, spaced out at about 5 cm. With a pastry brush dipped in water, lightly moisten the edges of the ravioli so the pastry cover will stick. Cover with another pasta sheet, press down really well, then cut the ravioli in a round or square shape. They should be about 8–10 cm in diameter. Make sure they are well sealed all round.

Lightly flour a tray and place the ravioli on it in a single layer. (At this stage they can be frozen, if you are not using them on the day.) Drop the ravioli into a pan of boiling, salted water. Cook the ravioli for about 2–3 minutes, or until al dente. Remove them one at a time and arrange 3–4 on individual dishes.

Heat the butter over medium heat until it bubbles, then add the sage and cook until crisp. Sprinkle parmigiano over the ravioli and pour the bubbling butter and sage sauce over them.

Variation

You can also use the tomato sauce on page 26.

Salsa al Pomodoro

Tomato Sauce

Serves 4–6

1 Spanish onion, chopped

25 g unsalted butter

25 ml good-quality virgin olive oil

2–3 cloves garlic, chopped

6–8 anchovies

a few sage leaves

1 bay leaf

150 g tomato paste

500 g ripe, peeled roma tomatoes (canned tomatoes can be used if fresh are not available)

salt and ground black pepper

1 small chilli (optional)

a few basil leaves, for serving

This is a classic and basic tomato sauce. You can use it to accompany pasta, on pizza, or with eggs or meat.

Soften the onion in the butter and olive oil. Add the garlic, anchovies, sage and bay leaf (or you can use thyme, oregano or rosemary if you prefer).

Add the tomato paste and stir well, cooking until the paste turns a terracotta colour (do not let it burn). Add the tomatoes, mix well, season as required and add the chilli, if using.

Cover and cook for about 20 minutes, stirring often. Finally, chop the basil leaves and add to the dish.

Note

The tomato paste gives the sauce a richer, stronger flavour.

Bottarga con Sedano

Smoked Fish Roe with Celery

Serves 6

roe of 1 smoked mullet
  (bottarga)

6–8 celery stalks

juice of ½ organic lemon

good-quality virgin olive
  oil, for drizzling

ground black pepper

Bottarga, dried roe of mullet, is a prized ingredient in Sardinia and Sicily. The combination of the salty, fishy flavour of the bottarga with the fresh crunchiness of the celery is inspired.

Peel off the very thin outer membrane of the mullet roe as it can be bitter.

Slice the celery stalks very thinly and arrange on individual dishes. Over the top of the celery, slice the bottarga very thinly.

Squeeze over the lemon juice, then a drizzle of virgin olive oil and some pepper and serve.

Note

You can buy this fish roe at the fish markets or at your fishmonger. The two long egg sacks are vacuum packed, so they will keep for a few weeks in the fridge.

Involtini di Melanzane

Rolled Eggplant

Serves 6

3 firm young eggplants
(aubergines)

600 ml peanut oil, for frying

2 large fresh mozzarella
balls

20 anchovies fillets in oil,
drained

1 handful fresh basil leaves

salt and ground black
pepper

You can serve this dish as part of an antipasto or as a first course.

Preheat the oven to 220°C (gas mark 7).

Slice the eggplants lengthways, about 5 mm thick – you need around 20 slices in total.

Heat the oil in a large frying pan and when it is very hot, fry the eggplant slices in batches, until golden. Remove them from the pan and drain on kitchen paper.

Cut each mozzarella ball in half then cut each half into 5 even slices. Top each slice of eggplant with an anchovy, a slice of mozzarella and a basil leaf. Season lightly with salt and pepper. Roll each slice up tightly and secure with a toothpick.

Butter a shallow ovenproof dish. Arrange the involtini in the dish and bake for 10 minutes, until the mozzarella begins to melt.

Peperoni con Acciughe

Capsicum with Anchovies

Serves 6

3 firm red capsicums
(peppers)

1 firm yellow capsicum
(pepper)

2–3 cloves garlic

fresh basil

15 anchovies

good-quality virgin olive oil,
for drizzling

You will find this dish in most Italian antipasti. Although it takes a little time to skin the capsicums, it is well worth it. They will have a delicious smoky flavour and be quite silky.

Blacken the skin of the capsicums over a flame (a gas burner on the stove or a kitchen blow torch), turning the capsicums over and over using tongs. When blackened, place them in a plastic bag, tie the top and let them cool for about 30 minutes.

After this time remove the skin, which should easily slide off. (The flesh of the capsicums should still be firm, not mushy.) Cut the capsicums in slices, removing cores and seeds, and dry them well with kitchen paper. Remove any remaining pieces of skin.

In a serving dish arrange a layer of capsicum then some chopped garlic, basil and some anchovy fillets. Continue layering until everything is used up. Now drizzle over some olive oil and let stand for a few hours before serving.

Polipini con Patate

Octopus with Potatoes

Serves 6

3–4 medium octopus

2 organic lemons

2–3 fresh bay leaves

1 kg yellow waxy potatoes, such as kipfler

250 ml good-quality virgin olive oil

salt and ground black pepper

a few sprigs flat-leaf parsley, finely chopped

I first tried this dish in a minuscule restaurant in Milan called La Latteria. It was across the road from the local newspaper, *Corriere della sera*. The owner told me that journalists in Milan are very fussy and partial to their food. Apparently this dish was a favourite.

Cut the heads off the octopus and discard. Bring a pan of water to the boil, add ½ lemon, sliced, and the bay leaves. Add the octopus and boil gently over medium heat for about 20 minutes. Allow to cool in the water.

Boil the potatoes and when cooked, cut into bite-sized pieces.

Pull off the octopus tentacles, remove the slimy skin and cut the flesh into bite-sized pieces. Add to the potatoes. Mix together the juice of the remaining 1½ lemons with the olive oil, salt, pepper and parsley. Pour this mixture over the octopus and potatoes. Serve at room temperature.

Pomodorini al Forno

Baked Cherry Tomatoes

Serves 4

2 tablespoons good-quality
   virgin olive oil

20–25 very ripe, vine-
   ripened cherry or small
   tomatoes

10 fresh basil leaves

1 teaspoon fresh thyme

sea salt flakes

3–4 garlic cloves, sliced

ground black pepper

Baking the tomatoes concentrates their flavour and the finished dish looks brilliantly colourful and inviting.

Preheat the oven to 220°C (gas mark 7).

Add the olive oil to a large ovenproof dish, then add the tomatoes, still attached to their stalks. Add the basil, thyme, salt, garlic and pepper.

Place in the oven and cook for about 15–20 minutes. Serve warm or cold. I like to serve these with Polpettone (page 319) instead of the tomato sauce. But they are equally delicious eaten with Pesce Spada al Salmoriglio (page 57).

Pomodori Ripieni

Stuffed Tomatoes

Serves 4

8 firm, ripe, medium-sized
  tomatoes

50 g unsalted butter

60 ml good-quality virgin
  olive oil

1 medium Spanish onion,
  very finely diced

10 anchovy fillets in oil,
  drained and chopped

2 tablespoons capers in
  brine, drained and chopped

2 handfuls flat-leaf parsley,
  chopped

75 g fresh breadcrumbs

50 g pine nuts, toasted

2 handfuls fresh basil
  leaves, chopped

salt and ground black
  pepper

Preheat the oven to 160°C (gas mark 3).

With a sharp knife, slice the tops off the tomatoes. (If you like, you can reserve the tops to put back on the tomatoes before baking.) Use a small spoon to scoop out just the seeds, leaving the fleshy internal chambers intact. Arrange the tomatoes upside down on a rack and leave to drain for about 30 minutes.

Meanwhile, melt the butter and half the oil in a large frying pan. Add the onion and fry gently until soft. Add the anchovies, capers and parsley and cook for just a few minutes. Add the remaining oil and the breadcrumbs and fry gently for a few minutes more, taking care not to burn the breadcrumbs. Add the pine nuts and basil, and season with a little salt and pepper.

Stuff the mixture into the tomatoes, making sure you press it gently into all the internal chambers. Replace the tomato 'lids', if using, then arrange the tomatoes on an oven tray and bake for around an hour. The tomatoes can be eaten hot or cold.

Acciughe Fresche

Fresh Anchovies

Serves 6–8

8–16 fresh anchovies

40 g breadcrumbs

1–2 cloves garlic, crushed

1 chilli, finely chopped

1 handful finely chopped
  flat-leaf parsley

salt and ground black
  pepper

good-quality virgin olive oil,
  for drizzling

Fresh anchovies have a much more delicate flavour than the salted variety. You can ask your fishmonger to clean them, as the job is a bit fiddly.

I also like to squeeze lemon juice over the cooked anchovies, especially when I eat them cold.

Preheat the oven to 220°C (gas mark 7).

Split open the anchovies down the belly, then remove the heads and spines. Rinse them under running water and dry with kitchen paper. Lay the fish flat, belly side down and spread open, on kitchen paper.

Put the breadcrumbs, garlic, chilli, parsley, salt and pepper in a bowl and stir together with a spoon.

Oil an ovenproof serving dish. Sprinkle some of the breadcrumb mixture evenly, but not too thickly, over the bottom of the dish. Arrange the anchovies, in a single layer, in the dish. Sprinkle some more breadcrumb mix on top and then drizzle some olive oil all over the fish.

Cook in the oven for about 5 minutes, until the fish are slightly coloured. Serve either hot or cold.

Antipasto di Cozze

Grilled Mussels

Serves 4

1 kg mussels (about
  6–8 mussels per person)

100 g breadcrumbs

2 cloves garlic, chopped

1 handful finely chopped
  flat-leaf parsley

50 ml good-quality virgin
  olive oil

salt and ground black
  pepper

Clean the mussels under cold, running water and pull or cut away their beards.

Heat about 125 ml water in a large saucepan. When boiling, add the mussels, cover the pan and let them cook until the shells open – shake the pan from time to time. (The mussels will take about 5 minutes to open.) When they are cool enough to handle, arrange them in an ovenproof dish, using only one half of the shell (discard the other halves).

Preheat the grill to high.

In a bowl, mix together the breadcrumbs, garlic, parsley, olive oil, salt and pepper to a crumbly paste. Place a little of this mixture on every half mussel shell, pressing down well around the mussel.

Cook under the hot grill for a few minutes until the topping starts to colour but not burn. This dish can be eaten hot or cold.

Insalata di Finocchi

Fennel Salad

Serves 4

2 fennel bulbs
  (use the longer, thinner
  male fennel bulb)

juice of 1 organic lemon

125 ml good-quality virgin
  olive oil

1 tablespoon wholegrain
  Dijon mustard

salt and ground black
  pepper

1 tablespoon capers

I like to use the male fennel, which is slightly longer in shape and thinner. I find them more tender.

Cut the fennel bulb in half lengthways and slice as thinly as possible. Mix the remaining ingredients together well to make a sauce and pour over the fennel. Chop some of the fennel's fine green leaves and sprinkle over the salad.

Note

This is a very fresh and crunchy salad ideally served with fish – for instance Pesce al Sale (page 161) – as one of the vegetables, or you can serve it as part of an antipasto.

Insalata di Cavolfiore

Cauliflower Salad

Serves 4

1 small, firm white
  cauliflower, leaves removed
  and divided into small
  florets

125 ml red-wine vinegar

250 ml good-quality virgin
  olive oil

4–5 anchovy fillets, mashed

1 fresh chilli, finely chopped

1 handful flat-leaf parsley,
  chopped

I love this salad. The crunchy flavour of the cauliflower, the salty sharpness of the anchovies and the heat of the chillies go really well together.

Put some salted water in a saucepan and bring to the boil. Drop the cauliflower florets into the water and boil for a few minutes – they should still be very firm. Rinse them under cold water to prevent them from cooking further, then dry on kitchen paper.

In a bowl mix the red-wine vinegar with the olive oil then add the anchovies and chilli. Pour this mixture over the cauliflower and sprinkle with the chopped parsley. Serve this salad as part of an antipasto or with grilled meats.

Carpaccio di Zucchine

Zucchini Salad

Serves 4

juice of 1 organic lemon

125 ml good-quality virgin olive oil

salt and ground black pepper

1 small fresh chilli, deseeded and finely chopped (optional)

3–4 small young zucchini (courgettes), thinly sliced

In my vegetable garden, which I can see from my kitchen window, I can spot the moment when the zucchini are at their summer peak. I pick them every second day as they grow quickly and do need to be especially small and very fresh for this simple salad. When you buy zucchini make sure they are small and very firm.

To make the dressing, mix together the lemon juice, olive oil, salt, pepper and chilli. Pour over the zucchini and allow to rest for about 15 minutes before serving. I like to serve this dish with a frittata (page 35).

Caponatina

Serves 6

1 kg small, young eggplants
  (aubergines)

250–375 ml good-quality
  virgin olive oil

2 red capsicums (peppers),
  thinly sliced

1 large Spanish onion, sliced

2–3 celery stalks, sliced

2 carrots, diced

10 anchovy fillets in
  oil, drained

250 g tomato paste

400 g canned roma tomatoes

75 ml red-wine vinegar

1 tablespoon sugar

75 g green olives, pitted

2 tablespoons pine nuts,
  lightly toasted

1 large handful flat-leaf
  parsley, chopped

salt and ground black
  pepper

1 large handful fresh basil
  leaves, chopped

In Sicily every mamma seems to have her own recipe for
caponatina and, of course, hers is always the best. So, at the
risk of being controversial, here is mine.

Cut the eggplants into 2 cm cubes. (If you use small, young
eggplants you do not need to salt them to draw out the
bitterness.)

Heat 200 ml of the olive oil in a large saucepan. Fry the
eggplant cubes in batches until they are pale gold all over. Remove
from the pan with a slotted spoon and drain on kitchen paper.

If necessary, add more oil to the pan then fry the capsicum
slices until they are soft. Remove from the pan and drain on
kitchen paper.

Add a little more oil to the pan and fry the onion, celery and
carrots until soft, but not coloured. Add the anchovies and tomato
paste and cook for 5–10 minutes, until the mixture turns a rich,
dark red. Add the canned tomatoes and cook for 15 minutes over
a low heat, stirring from time to time. Stir in the vinegar and
sugar and cook for 10 minutes. Add the olives, pine nuts and
parsley, together with the eggplant and capsicum. Cook for
10 more minutes then remove from the heat and leave to cool.

Just before serving, taste and adjust the seasoning to your
liking then stir in the basil. Serve at room temperature or cold.

Cipolline Tonnate

Onions with Tuna Mayonnaise

Serves 4

good-quality virgin olive oil,
  for drizzling

10 small onions, peeled

Vitello Tonnato sauce
  (page 166)

I like to use these delicious sweet onions when I make vitello tonnato. They are exceptional with the tuna–mayonnaise sauce. Of course, you can also use them on their own or as part of an antipasto.

Preheat the oven to 190°C (gas mark 5).

Drizzle the olive oil over the onions and put them on an oven tray. Bake until they are cooked, shaking the tray from time to time – about 20 minutes.

When cool arrange them in a serving dish and pour the Vitello Tonnato mayonnaise over them.

Finocchio al Forno

Baked Fennel

Serves 4

125 ml good-quality virgin
   olive oil

6 fennel bulbs, quartered
   (use the long, thin, male
   fennel bulbs)

2 Spanish onions, quartered

salt and ground black
   pepper

1 bunch flat-leaf parsley,
   finely chopped

When you bake fennel and Spanish onions together, there is a wonderful exchange of flavours. This dish can be eaten hot or cold.

Preheat the oven to 200°C (gas mark 6).

Drizzle 2 tablespoons of the olive oil over the base of an ovenproof dish. Scatter in the fennel and onion, then add the rest of the oil and mix so that the vegetables are thoroughly coated.

Bake for about 20 minutes, shaking the dish from time to time to stop the vegetables from sticking to the bottom of the dish. They should start to colour lightly. Remove from the oven, season with salt and pepper and stir in the parsley before serving.

Variation

I sometimes like to sprinkle on 3 tablespoons fresh breadcrumbs and 4 tablespoons freshly grated parmigiano before baking.

Pesce al Sale

Fish in a Salt Crust

Serves 6

1 whole 1.5–2 kg fish
(such as red emperor,
snapper or any other firm
white-fleshed fish), gutted
and cleaned but with the
scales left on

organic lemon slices

fennel, sliced (or bay
leaves, tarragon or thyme,
if preferred)

2 kg fine salt

water

DRESSING

juice of 1 organic lemon

175 ml good-quality virgin
olive oil

salt and ground black
pepper

My friend Tito, who has a restaurant (one of my very favourites) in San Pantaleo, a village in the hills above the Costa Smeralda in Sardinia, taught me this recipe. It is such a festive dish, which appears in a theatrical flourish at the table to delight your guests. Although the fish is totally covered with salt, it forms a crust that does not penetrate the scales so the fish inside is not salty.

The scales will stick to the salt and, when the crust is cracked, peel off like a glove, leaving the fish inside beautifully moist and cooked in its own juices.

Preheat the oven to 200°C (gas mark 6).

Place the fish in an oiled baking dish and insert some lemon and fennel slices into its stomach cavity.

In a bowl mix the salt with a little water – just enough to make the salt sticky. Cover the fish thickly with the salt, making sure it is well sealed everywhere (see Note). Bake in the oven for about 40 minutes.

Mix together the fresh lemon juice and olive oil to serve as a dressing over the fish.

When serving the fish, break the salt crust at the table, in front of your guests, as it looks impressive. Make sure you remove all the salt crust before eating – usually the skin of the fish will come off easily with the crust.

Note

If the fish is very large, don't cover its head with salt so you will have enough to cover the body properly.

Spiedini di Pesce Spada

Swordfish Kebabs

Serves 6

1 kg swordfish, cut into
  2.5 cm cubes

fresh bay leaves

MARINADE

2 cloves garlic

1 chilli

sea salt flakes

juice of ½ organic lemon

250 ml good-quality virgin
  olive oil

Salsa Verde (page 103)

Swordfish lends itself very well to kebabs as it has a firm flesh.

String the fish cubes onto wooden or steel skewers (if using wooden skewers, soak them first in water, so that they will not burn on the grill). After every third fish cube add a fresh bay leaf on the skewer.

In a mortar, mix all the marinade ingredients together well. Pour this marinade over the fish skewers and let rest for about 15 minutes.

Preheat the grill to high.

Grill the fish under a very hot grill for about 3–4 minutes, turning the skewers so that the fish is nicely coloured all over. Serve with the salsa verde.

Tonno sott'Olio

Tuna in Oil

Serves 6

1 piece fresh tuna, about
  1 kg

1 litre good-quality virgin
  olive oil

200 ml grapeseed oil
  (see Note)

4–5 fresh bay leaves

fresh thyme

whole peppercorns

1–2 chillies

COURT BOUILLON

1–2 celery stalks and
  leaves, cut in pieces

1–2 cloves garlic

3 cloves

1 large onion, cut into
  pieces

1 teaspoon whole
  peppercorns

3–4 teaspoons salt

This is a classic way to preserve tuna that was used before tuna canneries were established.

A word of warning: if you make this tuna, you will never buy tinned tuna again. This is just too delicious.

Place all the court bouillon ingredients in about 2 litres water and boil for about 30 minutes, to release all the flavours. Now add the tuna to the bouillon and cook for about 15 minutes on low heat. (The timing depends a bit on the thickness of the piece of tuna – it has to be only just cooked.)

Let the tuna cool in the court bouillon for about 3 hours. Take it out, remove the skin and dry well with kitchen paper.

Put the tuna in a glass jar or dish, cover with the olive and grapeseed oils plus the bay leaves, thyme, peppercorns and chillies.

Refrigerate for 48 hours before use.

Note
The grapeseed oil is essential, as it prevents the olive oil from solidifying when the tuna is refrigerated. The tuna will keep for up to 10 days in the refrigerator.

Vitello Tonnato
Veal with Tuna Mayonnaise

Serves 6

1 veal nut (noix or topside),
  wrapped very tightly
  in cheesecloth (muslin)

250 ml dry white wine

1–2 large carrots, cut into
  large pieces

1–2 celery stalks, cut into
  large pieces

1 large onion, cut into
  large pieces

2 bay leaves

a few peppercorns

MAYONNAISE

2 organic egg yolks

1 teaspoon salt

1 teaspoon Dijon mustard

300 ml sunflower oil

juice of ½ organic lemon

salt and ground black
  pepper

TUNA MIX

500 g canned tuna

20 anchovies in oil

1 handful capers, plus
  extra for garnish

salt and ground black
  pepper

Choose a saucepan that the veal will just fit into. Place the veal in the pan and cover with cold water. Add the wine, carrots, celery, onion, bay leaves and peppercorns. Put the lid on. Bring to the boil and then reduce the heat to low. Let it simmer for 20–25 minutes. Allow the meat to cool in the stock (see Note).

For the mayonnaise, beat the egg yolks with the salt and mustard then, while continuing to beat steadily, add the oil drop by drop – as the yolks begin to thicken, increase the oil to a steady trickle. Add some lemon juice then more oil, alternating until you have used up both the oil and lemon juice. Season to taste.

Place the tuna, anchovies and capers in a food processor, pulse to mix and add 1–2 ladlefuls of the veal stock. The tuna mixture should be like a thick cream. Taste and add salt and pepper if needed.

Slice the veal very thinly and arrange on a serving plate. Mix some of the mayonnaise with the tuna mixture and spread some of it over the sliced meat and put the rest in a bowl, to serve on the side. Garnish with capers.

Note
The left-over stock from cooking the veal can be used to make risotto. It can also be frozen for later use.

Pollo Capriccioso

Capricious Chicken

Serves 6

5 organic chicken breasts

25 ml virgin olive oil

sea salt flakes and ground
black pepper

1 red capsicum (pepper)

1 yellow capsicum (pepper)

2–3 carrots

2–3 celery stalks

baby iceberg lettuce or
radicchio leaves, for
serving

400 ml home-made
mayonnaise (see page
166), made extra lemony

1 handful rocket leaves

½ cup toasted pine nuts

MARINADE

125 ml good-quality virgin
olive oil

125 ml lemon juice

2–3 cloves garlic, chopped

1 chilli, chopped

2–3 fresh bay leaves,
chopped

This dish looks absolutely spectacular. Serve it in a large,
long dish and put it in the middle of the table for people to
help themselves.

Mix together all the marinade ingredients, pour over the chicken
breasts and leave for about 30 minutes.

Preheat the oven to 200°C (gas mark 6).

Heat a large cast-iron griddle or pan, add the olive oil and sear
the chicken breasts to brown them, then finish off in the oven for
about 20 minutes, or until done. Let them cool, then cut into 2 cm
strips. Season with salt and pepper.

Cut all the vegetables into thin sticks.

On your serving dish, arrange some baby iceberg or radicchio
leaves. Mix the carrots and celery with 125 ml mayonnaise. Spoon
onto the leaves then add the capsicum followed by the chicken
pieces. Put the rocket leaves on top of the chicken and, finally,
scatter over the pine nuts. Serve the remainder of the mayonnaise
on the side.

Addas Polo ba Bareh

Spiced Lamb and Rice

Serves 8

500 g Iranian rice or basmati long-grain rice

150 g small brown lentils

1½ teaspoons salt

1 organic egg yolk

175 ml thick plain yoghurt

125 g melted unsalted butter, plus extra unmelted butter

250 g lamb fillet, chopped in small pieces

1 Spanish onion, chopped

2 cloves garlic, chopped

1 teaspoon ground turmeric

2 teaspoons ground cumin

1 teaspoon ground cinnamon

½ teaspoon ground nutmeg

pomegranate seeds, to serve (optional)

This 'polo' (the Iranian word for rice) brings back wonderful memories for me. I spent the first eight years of my life in Persia. My mother would prepare this rice dish in summer. The whole family would gather outside to eat it, seated on a large Persian carpet, the stars overhead and fireflies flickering in the darkness.

I know it's not really Italian, but it is a great summer experience so I decided to slip it in anyway.

Rinse the rice well in cold water 2–3 times.

Bring 2 litres salted water to the boil, add the rice and parboil it for about 5 minutes, then drain.

Cover the lentils with cold water, add the salt and bring to the boil. Cook for about 20 minutes. (The lentils should still be a little al dente.) Drain and set aside.

Mix 150 g of the rice with the egg yolk, yoghurt and melted butter. Put this in a non-stick, buttered heavy pan, and set aside.

In another pan, melt a little butter and cook the lamb, onion and garlic until the lamb has browned and the onion softened – about 5 minutes. Add all the spices.

Now mix the remaining parboiled plain rice and the lentils with the lamb mixture and pile it on top of the yoghurt and rice mixture in a large pan. With a wooden spoon handle, make holes in the rice and add some small pieces of butter. Put the lid on tight and, over a very low heat, cook for about 30–40 minutes.

To serve, turn it upside down onto a warm dish. The rice should have a beautiful golden crust on top.

Sorbetto al Pompelmo Rosa con Campari

Pink Grapefruit and Campari Sorbet

Serves 6–8

4–5 large pink grapefruits, juiced

125 g caster sugar

125 ml Campari

5 drops Angostura bitters

The bitterness of the Campari, grapefruit and Angostura gives this sorbet a quite unusual flavour. It is such a refreshing dessert, perfect to be eaten on a hot summer's evening.

Mix all the ingredients together well. When the sugar has completely dissolved, put into an ice cream machine and churn until fluffy and light coloured.

Spoon the sorbet into glasses and finish off with a little more Campari on top. The sorbet should not be too sweet.

Granita al Limone

Lemon Granita

Serves 6

5 organic lemons

3 lemon leaves

200 g caster sugar

200 ml water

Use a sharp knife to peel 3 thick, long strips of zest from the lemons. Squeeze the lemons and reserve the juice.

Place the zest in a saucepan with the lemon leaves, sugar and water and simmer gently for about 5 minutes. Remove from the heat and leave to cool before straining. Stir the lemon juice into the syrup. Pour into an ice cream machine and churn until it has a light and fluffy texture.

If you don't have an ice cream machine, pour the mixture into a shallow metal tray and place in the freezer. Every 1–2 hours take it out of the freezer and stir with a fork to mix the frozen crystals back into the liquid. When the granita is completely frozen, break it up roughly and place in a food processor. Pulse briefly until it is light and fluffy then return to the freezer until ready to serve.

Spoon the granita into glasses and serve.

Note

This granita is quite tart, which is the way I like it. If you prefer it sweeter, just add a little more sugar.

Granita al Gelso

Mulberry Granita

Serves 4

300 g ripe, dark-red
  mulberries

juice of 1 organic lemon

125 g caster sugar

100 ml water

whipped cream, to serve

This granita is the most intense dark-red colour and looks spectacular topped with whipped cream.

Place all the ingredients except the cream into a food processor and blend to a smooth purée. Pour into an ice cream machine and churn until it has a light and fluffy texture.

If you don't have an ice cream machine, pour the mixture into a shallow metal tray and place in the freezer. Every 1–2 hours take it out of the freezer and stir with a fork to mix the frozen crystals back into the liquid. When the granita is completely frozen, break it up roughly and place in a food processor. Pulse briefly until it is light and fluffy then return to the freezer until ready to serve.

Spoon the granita into glasses and top with whipped cream.

Sorbetto al Ananas

Pineapple Sorbet

Serves 6

1 large ripe pineapple,
skinned and cored

60 g caster sugar

100 ml water

Cut the pineapple into pieces, place it in a food processor and process until smooth.

Make a syrup with the sugar and water and, when cool, add to the pineapple purée. Taste to see if if it sweet enough and add more sugar if necessary. Churn the mixture in an ice cream machine until fluffy.

Variation

You can add 3–4 finely chopped fresh mint leaves before putting the mixture into the ice cream machine.

Gello di Anguria

Watermelon Jelly

Serves 6

2 kg ripe watermelon

120 g caster sugar

50 g cornflour

1 tablespoon jasmine
water (see Note),
or 1 teaspoon rosewater

1 teaspoon ground
cinnamon

50 g dark chocolate, grated

50 g unsalted pistachio
nuts, finely chopped

jasmine flowers or rose
petals, to garnish
(optional)

Slice the watermelon flesh away from the skin and remove all the seeds. Place in a blender and process to a smooth purée – one 2 kg watermelon should yield around 1 litre watermelon purée.

Mix the sugar, cornflour and jasmine water (or rosewater) with a little of the watermelon purée to make a smooth paste. Stir in the remaining watermelon purée and tip the mixture into a saucepan. Bring to the boil slowly over a gentle heat. The mixture will start to thicken. When it does, remove the pan from the heat and stir in the cinnamon.

Pour the jelly into individual small moulds or one large mould, which you have moistened with a little water. Leave to set in the refrigerator for several hours or, better still, overnight.

To serve, loosen the jelly by submerging the mould in warm water for a few seconds. Invert it onto a serving platter and decorate with grated chocolate, chopped pistachio nuts and jasmine flowers or rose petals.

Note

To make jasmine water, soak 10 fresh jasmine flowers overnight in 50 ml water. The next day, strain the water and use within 24 hours.

Crostata di Datteri

Date Tart

Serves 8

PASTRY

125 g unsalted butter

200 g unbleached plain flour

60 g sugar

pinch of salt

zest of 1 organic lemon
and few drops of juice

FILLING

125 g unsalted butter

125 g coconut cream

125 g brown sugar

pinch of salt

50 ml Nocino (walnut
liqueur), or Mirto liqueur
(optional)

approximately 30 dried
dates, pitted and cut
lengthways

Process all the pastry ingredients in a food processor. Roll out and lay in a 28 cm springform pan. Place in the freezer for about 30 minutes.

Preheat the oven to 200°C (gas mark 6).

Remove the pastry from the freezer, prick the base with a fork then blind bake in the oven until lightly coloured – about 15 minutes.

Mix together all the filling ingredients, except the dates, and boil in a pan for 20 minutes. Allow to cool.

When the pastry is cool, arrange the dates in a fan shape on top of the pastry. Pour the cooled sauce over the dates (if the sauce is too hot, it will be too liquid and soften the pastry).

Serve with whipped cream.

Autunno

AUTUMN

Autunno

If I had to choose my favourite season for Italian food, it would have to be autumn. After a long summer the cooler days begin and a remarkable range of produce becomes available.

My autumn would be enjoyed in Piemonte, in Italy's north-west, an area that, even by Italian standards, has an extraordinary variety of wonderful foods that come to a sort of crescendo in autumn. Culturally the range is great, with traditional peasant food of extreme simplicity contrasting with the sophistication found in Turin, the capital city of the Dukes of Savoy (who later became the royal family of Italy).

Autumn in Piemonte is spectacular. Fresh cheeses are brought down from the mountain pastures, the rice harvest is under way in the Po Valley, porcini mushrooms can be found in the woods, hazelnuts are being picked and wine grapes are ripening in the Langhe wine region. The high point of the season is the arrival of wild white truffles in October.

My list of autumn recipes has peasant dishes like Bagna Caoda, Uova in Salsa Verde and Uova alla Diavola. At the other extreme, but also simple, is a recipe for grated white truffles served with plain pasta and butter. There are recipes for porcini mushrooms with potatoes and a veal recipe from the Val d'Aosta. There are three recipes using Po Valley rice varieties and two great veal recipes – Sottilina and Rotolo di Vitello – which could have been favourites at the Savoy Court in Turin.

The real indulgences of the sophisticated city-dwellers show most in the desserts. Chocolate arrived early in Turin (it is said in the dowry of a Spanish princess) and was combined, in a stroke of inspiration, with the local hazelnuts. Chocolate and hazelnuts are used in desserts, cakes and ice creams and I have included some of these recipes.

Rotolini Salati

Rolled Savoury Biscuits

Makes 15 biscuits

1 sheet butter puff pastry
(see Note)

FILLING 1

4 thin slices good-quality
  prosciutto

50 g grated parmigiano

ground black pepper

FILLING 2

125 g grated Gruyère

ground black pepper

8 anchovy fillets

FILLING 3

1–2 cloves garlic, crushed

140 g tomato paste

2–3 mozzarella bocconcini,
  thinly sliced (if you prefer
  you can use parmigiano,
  Gruyère or another cheese)

4–5 fresh basil or
  10 oregano leaves, chopped

salt and ground black
  pepper

Piemonte is famous for small savoury nibbles (called stuzzichini)
to go with aperitivi, drinks before dinner. Here are some of
my favourites.

Preheat the oven to 200°C (gas mark 6).

FOR FILLING 1

Lay the prosciutto slices on the pastry, then sprinkle the cheese
and pepper evenly over the prosciutto. Roll the pastry, as tightly
as possible, into the shape of a sausage. With a very sharp knife,
cut the sausage into slices about 1 cm wide.

Put some greaseproof paper on an oven tray, arrange the little
rolled biscuits evenly on the tray, side by side, and cook in the
oven until golden brown, about 5–8 minutes.

These biscuits are delicious eaten hot, but they can also be
eaten at room temperature.

FOR FILLING 2

Sprinkle the cheese and pepper evenly over the pastry. Then
arrange the anchovy fillets widthways in two rows, about 10 cm
apart. Roll the pastry sheet up into a sausage, making sure that
the anchovies are lying across the sheet, so that when you cut the
sausage, every slice gets a piece of anchovy. Proceed to slice and
cook as directed above.

FOR FILLING 3

Spread the filling ingredients over the pastry, ensuring the
bocconcini is evenly distributed, then roll, slice and cook as above.

Note

With these puff pastry rolls you can really let your imagination
run wild. You can use any filling that takes your fancy – I have
provided some of my favourites. To make things easier, I suggest
you buy butter puff pastry at the supermarket.

Grissini con le Olive

Bread Sticks with Olives

Serves 6

DOUGH

300 g unbleached plain
flour, preferably Italian
type 00

200 g rye flour

1½ tablespoons dry yeast

1 teaspoon malt extract

1½ teaspoons salt

375 ml warm water

60 ml good-quality virgin
olive oil

2 tablespoons lard (optional,
although the lard gives
the grissini extra flavour)

125 g green olives, pitted

unbleached plain flour or
semolina, for dusting

good-quality virgin olive oil,
for brushing

sea salt

Preheat the oven to 240°C (gas mark 9).

Mix all the dough ingredients together and knead until the dough becomes shiny and elastic. Make sure the dough is not too dry – add a few more drops of warm water if necessary.

Shape the dough into a ball and put in a lightly oiled bowl. Put a few drops of oil over the dough, so that it does not dry out. Cover with a cloth and let it stand in a warm place for 1–2 hours.

Now punch the dough down and knead again, to get rid of all the air. Shape the dough roughly into a sausage about 10 cm in diameter, and cut slices off about 3 cm wide.

Take a slice of dough and arrange the olives in a row, touching each other. Now pinch the top of the dough together with your fingers in order to seal the olives in. Put a little flour or semolina on the workbench and roll the dough into a long grissino, about as thick as your finger.

Arrange the grissini on a baking tray, and let them stand for about 30 minutes. With a pastry brush, brush some more olive oil on them, and sprinkle them with salt.

Bake in the hot oven for about 5 minutes. Check them from time to time to make sure they do not burn.

Acciughe al Verde

Anchovies with Salsa Verde

Serves 4

20 very good quality
anchovies in oil

3 cloves garlic, unpeeled

1 bunch flat-leaf parsley

1 handful fresh basil leaves

1 small hot chilli, deseeded

2 hardboiled egg yolks

175 ml good-quality virgin
olive oil

juice of ½ organic lemon

Anchovies are a feature of Piemontese cooking. This dish can be served with drinks or as a starter.

Drain off the oil from the anchovies and pat them dry on kitchen paper, removing any largish bones.

Place the garlic cloves in water, bring to the boil and cook for 3 minutes. This will ensure their flavour is mild and sweet. Squeeze the garlic out of their skins, put into a food processor with all other ingredients, except the anchovies, and process until smooth and fluffy. (This salsa verde should have a thickish consistency.)

Put a little of the sauce on a serving dish, arrange some anchovies in a layer over it, then cover those anchovies with some more sauce. Continue in this way until all the anchovies and sauce have been used up. Let the dish stand at room temperature for 1–2 hours or longer, so the flavours can meld.

Serve as an antipasto with lots of crunchy, fresh bread, spread with a generous coating of unsalted butter.

Pâté di Tonno

Tuna Pâté

Serves 6

150 g unsalted butter

1 large Spanish onion, chopped

1 large shallot, chopped

1 bay leaf

2 sprigs fresh tarragon, finely chopped

10 anchovy fillets, finely chopped

125 ml oloroso sherry

400 g canned tuna in oil, drained

ground black pepper

This is a dish created by my grandfather, a famous restaurateur. It was his way of creating a simpler and lighter dish than the traditional pâté.

Using about 50 g of the butter, cook the onion and shallot until soft and transparent. Add the herbs and anchovies. After a few minutes add the sherry and let it evaporate. Add the remaining butter, cut into pieces, and let it melt gently, making sure it does not bubble.

Put the drained tuna and the butter mixture into a food processor, removing the bay leaf. Process for about 5–10 minutes, or until the mixture becomes a very pale colour. Taste for seasoning and add pepper if necessary.

Pour the mixture into a bowl and leave it in the refrigerator for about 2 hours, or until firm.

Variation

You can add 1–2 large boiled, mashed potatoes to the pâté to make it go further or lighten the taste.

Bagna Caoda della Mamma

Mamma's Raw Vegetables with Anchovy Cream

Serves 4–6

SAUCE

500 ml cream

4–6 cloves garlic (if you can find red garlic it will be sweeter)

50 g unsalted butter

8–10 anchovy fillets

ground black pepper

SELECTION OF VEGETABLES, SUCH AS:

1 Lebanese cucumber, peeled and sliced lengthways

2–3 carrots, cut lengthways

1 yellow and 1 red capsicum (pepper), deseeded and cut lengthways

3–4 celery stalks, cut lengthways

6–8 young cos (romaine) lettuce leaves

8–10 small button mushrooms

a few cauliflower florets

This is the way my mother used to make bagna caoda.

Boil the cream with the peeled garlic cloves for 15–20 minutes so that the cream reduces and thickens. In a fondue dish, melt the butter. Cut the anchovies very finely and add them to the butter. Cook them over a very gentle heat, until they have melted. Now add the reduced cream. Crush the softened garlic cloves with a fork and stir well, taste and add a little pepper.

Prepare the vegetables. Wash them well, slice, dry them, then put them on a large plate.

Put the sauce in a fondue dish over a flame in the centre of the table. Each person puts some vegetables on their plate, and then dips the vegetable sticks into the sauce. It is also delicious to serve some grissini on the side, to dip into the sauce (to make your own, see page 191).

Variation

The traditional method of preparing bagna caoda is to use a whole garlic head per person, boiled in a little milk until tender. The milk is discarded and the garlic peeled and mashed. Put it in a flameproof pot and add 50 g anchovies and 100 ml good-quality virgin olive oil per person.

Cook gently, without letting the mixture boil, for 20 minutes. Serve with raw capsicums (peppers) and cardoons.

P.S. Avoid all contact with other people for at least three days after eating this!

Tortine alla Ricotta

Ricotta and Parmesan Tarts

Makes 8 × 15 cm diameter tarts

PASTRY

500 g unbleached plain flour

200 g unsalted butter, at room temperature

2 organic eggs plus 1 egg yolk

100 g grated parmigiano

1 teaspoon salt

RICOTTA FILLING

1 kg ricotta

2 organic eggs

100 g grated parmigiano

1–2 teaspoons salt

ground black pepper

1 handful fresh oregano leaves

10 zucchini (courgette) flowers (optional), bitter stamens removed, roughly sliced

I find these ideal as a lunch dish. The combination of the ricotta and parmesan is light but very satisfying. They are wonderful served with a simple green salad.

Place all the pastry ingredients in a food processor and mix together to form a dough using a dough hook, but do not over-process. Put the dough in the refrigerator to rest for about 30–60 minutes.

In the meantime prepare the ricotta filling by mixing all the filling ingredients well in a bowl.

Preheat the oven to 200°C (gas mark 6) and butter 8 individual tartlet or pie dishes, or a 30 cm springform tin.

Divide the pastry dough into 8 pieces. Place between two sheets of greaseproof or baking paper and flatten the pastry until it is very thin. Line each tartlet mould with the pastry. Fill the individual tarts with the ricotta mixture – about 2 large spoonfuls each.

Bake in the preheated oven for about 20–25 minutes. When ready the ricotta should look puffed up and golden on top.

You can eat these tarts hot or at room temperature.

Bruco alla Fontina

Fontina Caterpillar

Serves 4–6

100 ml home-made
mayonnaise (page 166)

1 loaf ciabatta bread, sliced
but not right through – the
loaf should hold together

400 g Italian fontina, sliced
5 mm thick

12 anchovies

ground black pepper

This dish is a delicious way to use day-old bread. It was another favourite of my mother's. Its strong flavour comes from the cheese and anchovies, and the mayonnaise melts through the bread. The result is a crusty outside with a soft, deliciously gooey inside.

Preheat the oven to 200°C (gas mark 6).

Spread a little mayonnaise on each slice of bread. Slide a cheese slice between each bread slice along with an anchovy. Grind some pepper over the loaf. Put the loaf on some oiled aluminium foil and wrap the foil around the bread, leaving the top open, so that the loaf will crisp.

Cook the bread in the oven for about 20 minutes until golden-brown and crisp.

Note

Fontina is a mountain cheese that comes from the Val d'Aosta in Piemonte. It has quite a rich but delicate flavour and it melts beautifully when heated.

Frittata Gialla e Verde

Yellow and Green Frittata

Serves 4

6 organic eggs

salt and ground black
  pepper

25 g unsalted butter

1 bunch spinach, or a 250 g
  packet frozen spinach

4–5 slices prosciutto

4–5 tablespoons Pâté
  di Tonno (page 195)

Maria Teresa, a wonderful traditional Piemontese cook, showed
me how to prepare this frittata. The frittata comes out as a roll
that you slice to reveal the brilliant greenness of the spinach. It
looks very enticing. I serve this as a light lunch or as an entrée
for a special dinner.

Beat the eggs together until fluffy, then season with salt
and pepper.

Heat a large 35 cm pan, melt the butter in it and pour in
enough of the egg mixture to make a very thin frittata. Cook
over low heat until set, then remove from the pan.

If using frozen spinach, thaw it first and squeeze out all the
water. If using fresh spinach, blanch the leaves for 1 minute in
boiling, salted water, then squeeze out all the water and chop
roughly.

Arrange the prosciutto slices, side by side, on the frittata, then
spread the pâté di tonno over, about 1 cm thick, and finally the
spinach. Season with pepper and salt (be careful with the salt
as both the prosciutto and the pâté di tonno are already salted).

Now roll up the frittata like a swiss roll. Wrap the rolled
frittata in aluminium foil and refrigerate for at least 1 hour
or overnight.

To serve, unwrap the frittata and cut it into slices about 2 cm
thick. Serve as an antipasto or part of a larger antipasto platter.

Rotolo di Gnocchi con Spinaci

Gnocchi Roll with Spinach

Serves 6

2 kg floury potatoes, boiled

1–2 teaspoons salt

2 organic eggs, lightly beaten

200–300 g unbleached plain flour

100 g unsalted butter, cubed

10 fresh sage leaves

FILLING

250 g ricotta

50 g freshly grated parmigiano

1 organic egg

salt and ground black pepper

25 g unsalted butter

2 cloves garlic, crushed

250 g frozen spinach, thawed

While the potatoes are still hot, peel them and push them through a potato ricer. Now add the salt, eggs and, gradually, the flour. (The amount of flour will depend on the kind of potato you use, but remember that the less flour you use, the softer the gnocchi will be.) The gnocchi dough should be soft, but not stick to your hands.

With a rolling pin, roll out the dough until about 2 cm thick.

For the filling, mix the ricotta, parmigiano, egg, salt and pepper and spread this evenly on top of the dough. In a frying pan melt a little butter and lightly cook the garlic. Mix the thawed spinach with the butter and garlic, cook for just a few minutes and then spread this on top of the ricotta mixture.

Roll the gnocchi dough, ricotta and spinach into a sausage, swiss-roll style. Wrap the sausage tightly in cheesecloth (muslin). Tie each end and boil in salted water for about 10–15 minutes. Let it cool.

Preheat the oven to 200°C (gas mark 6).

Unwrap the roll gently from the cheesecloth and place it in a buttered oven dish that will hold the rotolo comfortably. With a sharp knife, cut the roll into slices about 2 cm thick. Sprinkle with some parmigiano, then dot cubed butter and sage leaves evenly over the slices. Cook in the oven until golden-brown, about 15 minutes.

Uova in Salsa Verde

Eggs on a Bed of Greens

Serves 1 as an antipasto or a light lunch

2 organic eggs per person

SAUCE

50 g unsalted butter

1–2 tablespoons good-quality virgin olive oil

1 small Spanish onion, chopped

2–3 cloves garlic, crushed

1 bunch flat-leaf parsley, chopped

2 tablespoons unbleached plain flour

water or vegetable stock, for thinning

salt and ground black pepper

This is a very simple dish with its origins in the 'cucina povera', or peasant cooking, of the countryside. It is simplicity with a delicious result, ideal as a lunch dish with crusty bread.

Boil the eggs for a maximum of 4–5 minutes, then leave to cool in cold water.

In a saucepan melt the butter with the olive oil and gently fry the onion and garlic (do not let them burn). Now add the parsley and cook for a few seconds only. Add the flour, let it cook for a few minutes, but do not let it brown or it will become bitter. Add some hot water or a light vegetable stock, stirring, until the sauce is the consistency of thick cream. Add salt and pepper to taste.

Shell the eggs, then cut them in half and put them cut side up in the sauce. Serve with some crunchy Italian bread.

Uova alla Diavola

Devilled Eggs

SAUCE

25 g unsalted butter

1–2 tablespoons good-
quality virgin olive oil

1 Spanish onion, finely
chopped

2–3 cloves garlic, crushed

a few fresh sage leaves

1 sprig fresh rosemary

1 fresh bay leaf

140 g tomato paste

500 g fresh, ripe, peeled
roma tomatoes (canned
ones will do)

salt and ground black
pepper

1 small chilli (optional),
chopped

1 tablespoon white vinegar

2 organic eggs per person

2 slices ciabatta bread
per person

a few fresh basil leaves

Melt the butter and oil and soften the onion and garlic until the onion becomes transparent, then add the sage, rosemary and bay leaf. Add the tomato paste and cook until the paste turns a terracotta colour. Add the peeled tomatoes, mix well, season and add the chilli. Cover and cook for about 20 minutes over low heat. The sauce for this dish should be strong and tasty.

Boil some water with the tablespoon of white vinegar and poach the eggs. Make sure that the yolks remain runny.

Toast or grill 2 slices of ciabatta bread per person. Arrange them on a plate and spoon 2–3 generous spoonfuls of tomato sauce on top. Then, making sure the poached eggs are drained of all water, place them on top of the sauce.

Chop the fresh basil, sprinkle it over the eggs and season with salt and pepper to taste.

Risotto alla Milanese

Milanese Risotto

Serves 6

2 litres well-flavoured fresh chicken or veal stock

1 large onion, chopped

125 g unsalted butter

50 ml good-quality virgin olive oil

bone marrow (optional, see Note)

pinch saffron

500 g carnaroli or arborio rice

300 ml dry white wine

125 g freshly grated parmigiano, plus extra for serving

salt and ground black pepper

fresh porcini mushrooms, pan-fried, for serving (optional)

This is one of the classics of Italian cooking. There are many variations but this is the basic recipe that inspired the others.

Allow the stock to come to the boil in a pan and then turn heat down and simmer.

In a large, heavy-based pan fry the onion in 50 g of the butter and the oil until transparent, then add the bone marrow and mix quickly. Add the saffron and then the rice. Coat the rice well with the oil, butter and marrow mix. Let it cook for 1–2 minutes then add the wine, stirring vigorously until it has evaporated. Add about half the stock to the rice and stir continuously over high heat. When the rice gets a bit dry, add more stock, this time one ladle at a time (the more stock you use the more flavour the risotto will have). After about 20 minutes the rice should be ready. It should still be a bit al dente.

Turn the heat off and add the remaining butter and about 70 g of the parmigiano, serving the rest on the side. Taste for salt and pepper and add if needed. Serve immediately with pan-fried porcini mushrooms, if you like.

Note

Ask the butcher to cut 2 large veal bones lengthways, so you will be able to remove the marrow. The marrow is optional in this recipe, but it does make the risotto taste fantastic.

Risotto con Rognoncini Triffolati

Risotto with Kidneys

Serves 6

Risotto alla Milanese
  (page 213)

ROGNONCINI

3 veal kidneys, skin and
  fat removed, diced

a little unbleached plain
  flour, for dusting

50 g unsalted butter

2 tablespoons good-quality
  virgin olive oil

1 Spanish onion, finely
  sliced

2 cloves garlic, crushed

8–10 fresh sage leaves

6 slices pancetta, diced

200 ml oloroso sherry

salt and ground black
  pepper

Make the Risotto alla Milanese but omit the bone marrow and saffron.

Dust the diced kidneys with flour.

In a heavy-based pan, melt the butter, add the oil and fry the onion, garlic, sage and pancetta until the onion is soft. Take care not to burn the garlic. Add the kidneys and, over fairly high heat, brown them quickly all over. Pour the sherry over the kidneys and, with a wooden spoon, scrape up all the bits on the bottom of the frying pan, so they are incorporated into the sauce. Season with salt and pepper. Put the lid on the pan, turn the heat to low and cook until the kidneys are done, about 15 minutes. If they look dry add a little more stock or sherry to the pan.

Pour the risotto into a serving dish, make a well in the top and fillit with the rognoncini plus all their juices. Serve immediately.

Note

Remember that risotto does not wait, so prepare the kidneys first if you think it might be too difficult having both cooking at the same time.

Riso in Cagnon

Rice with Sage and Parmigiano

Serves 4

350–400 g rice, preferably
  Vialone Nano variety
  (it does not fall apart
  and it keeps its bite)

50–75 g unsalted butter

2 cloves garlic

10 fresh sage leaves

100 g freshly grated
  parmigiano or fontina

This dish is perfect in its simplicity. By pouring the melted butter over the parmigiano, it will form a wonderful crust.

Boil the rice in salted water until cooked but still al dente.

Melt the butter in a frying pan, then add the garlic and the sage leaves. Let the butter bubble but do not burn it. Discard the garlic. The sage leaves should be crisp.

Pour the cooked rice on a serving dish. Sprinkle the cheese over the rice and then the bubbling hot butter and sage over the cheese. Serve immediately.

Taglierini al Burro e Tartufo Bianco

Taglierini with Butter and White Truffles

Serves 4

1 quantity tajerini (page 221)

80 g unsalted butter, melted

100 g freshly grated parmigiano

fresh white truffle or truffle oil, for garnish

White truffles are one of the high points of north Italian food. Unfortunately they cannot be cultivated outside their natural habitat in Piemonte. They grow in the wild and truffle hunters are notoriously secretive. The experience of the strong but delicate aroma of truffles is unique. To my taste they are best eaten when grated over something very simple to allow the aroma of the truffle to reign supreme.

When you can't get the truffles themselves, a little truffle oil can remind you of what they are really like.

Make the tajerini, then boil in plenty of salted water for just a few minutes. Drain the pasta and place it in a heated serving dish. Pour the melted butter over it, add the parmigiano and mix together.

If you have a fresh white truffle, shave it very thinly with a truffle slicer over the pasta, or alternatively drizzle over a few drops of truffle oil. Serve immediately.

Tajerini con Fegatini

Maria Teresa's Fresh Chicken Liver Tajerini

Serves 4

300–400 g very fine
  semolina flour

3–4 organic eggs

2 tablespoons good-quality
  virgin olive oil

1–2 teaspoons salt

SUGO DI FEGATINI

2 small onions, finely
  chopped

50 g unsalted butter

2 tablespoons good-quality
  virgin olive oil

250–300 g chicken livers,
  sinews and skin removed,
  roughly chopped

125 ml chicken stock

splash of dry Marsala
  or oloroso sherry

½ teaspoon sugar

salt

For these tajerini – thin, flat, fresh pasta ribbons that are called taglierini elsewhere in Italy – you need very fine semolina flour. The chicken liver sauce is a great accompaniment to them.

Mix the semolina, eggs, oil and salt together and knead until the mixture is well amalgamated and looks smooth and shiny. Cut a small piece of dough off and pass it through a pasta machine, fold it in three, and pass it through about 5–6 more times. Then reduce the width of the pasta machine until you get to number 2 or 3 (this depends a bit on your machine; the pasta should not be too thin).

Cut the pasta sheets to about 30 cm in length, and then cut them into tajerini ribbons (like spaghetti). Because this pasta is made with semolina it lasts much longer than other fresh pastas and will keep for up to 5 days in the refrigerator without becoming mouldy.

For the sauce (sugo), fry the onion in the butter and oil until transparent then add the chicken livers. After about 2–3 minutes add the chicken stock, cover and let it cook very gently for a few minutes, then add the Marsala and again let it cook for a few minutes. Season to taste with salt and sugar.

Boil the tajerini in lots of salted water – they will only take a minute or so to cook – drain well and then mix the sauce through the pasta. Serve immediately.

Timballo di Natalia

Natalia's Timballo

Serves 6

TOMATO SAUCE

25 g unsalted butter

2 tablespoons good-quality
   virgin olive oil

1 Spanish onion, very
   finely sliced

2 cloves garlic, very
   finely sliced

6 fresh sage leaves

2 sprigs fresh rosemary,
   stalks discarded

2 fresh bay leaves

140 g tomato paste

400 g canned roma tomatoes

salt and ground black
   pepper

500 ml sunflower oil,
   for frying

1 medium eggplant
   (aubergine), cut into
   small cubes

500 g anelli pasta (or other
   small pasta shapes of your
   choice, see Note)

2 tablespoons fresh
   breadcrumbs

1 large fresh mozzarella
   ball, cut into small cubes

Preheat the oven to 200°C (gas mark 6).

To make the sauce, heat the butter and oil in a large frying pan and gently fry the onion, garlic and herbs, taking care not to burn the garlic. When soft, add the tomato paste and cook for a few minutes, until the mixture darkens in colour. Stir in the tomatoes and cook over a gentle heat for about 20 minutes. Discard the bay leaves and season to your liking.

Heat the sunflower oil in a small frying pan and, when hot, fry the eggplant in batches until pale golden. Remove from the oil and drain on kitchen paper.

Cook the pasta in plenty of boiling, salted water until al dente. Drain well and mix in the tomato sauce so the pasta is evenly coated.

Thoroughly butter a round non-stick oven dish (25 cm in diameter and at least 8 cm deep). Sprinkle the breadcrumbs over the bottom and up the sides of the dish, then pour in half the pasta. Top with a layer of the eggplant and mozzarella, then cover with the remaining pasta. Bake for 15–20 minutes.

Remove from the oven and leave the timballo to stand for about 3 minutes before turning upside down onto a serving dish.

Note

This recipe uses a special pasta called anelli, shaped like little rings. You could also use farfalline, pennette or other small pasta shapes.

Cipolle Rosse al Forno

Baked Red Onions

Serves 6

12 medium Spanish onions, peeled (about 2 onions per person)

6 cloves garlic, very thinly sliced

1 bunch fresh thyme

175 g unsalted butter, at room temperature

salt and ground black pepper

I love to cook with Spanish onions. I find they are very sweet and not as strong as other varieties. They also lend themselves very well to being eaten raw in salads.

Preheat the oven to 180°C (gas mark 4).

Trim the base of the onions so that they can stand upright. Now cut a deep incision in the form of a cross on the top of the onions, making sure you do not cut right through them.

Stand the onions in an ovenproof dish. Put a few garlic slices and a few thyme leaves into the incisions. Mix the butter with the remaining thyme and garlic, and distribute it evenly among the onions, pushing the butter well into the onion. Season with salt and pepper. Cook in the oven for about 40 minutes.

Patate Arrosto con Funghi Porcini

Roast Potatoes with Porcini Mushrooms

Serves 4

1 kg waxy, yellow potatoes,
  such as Desiree

4 tablespoons good-quality
  virgin olive oil

100 g dried porcini
  mushrooms, soaked in
  750 ml warm water for
  15 minutes

about 12 cloves garlic,
  skin on

about 15 fresh sage leaves

100 g unsalted butter

sea salt flakes and ground
  black pepper

This dish is the essence of autumn – the season when you can find porcini mushrooms growing wild in the woods. When porcini and potatoes are cooked together, the potatoes absorb the earthy taste of the mushrooms and the whole dish takes on their wild woodland flavour.

Preheat the oven to 200°C (gas mark 6).

Peel and cut the potatoes into quarters. Choose a roasting pan that will hold the potatoes comfortably without crowding them and pour the olive oil into it. Add the potatoes and shake them around to coat with the oil.

Drain the porcini mushrooms, reserving the water they have been soaked in, and add them to the potatoes. Now mix the garlic and sage evenly through the potatoes and porcini. Add the water the porcini were soaked in and lastly chop the butter into small pieces and dot them around.

Roast in the oven for about 30 minutes, shaking the pan from time to time. The potatoes should be golden-brown and full of porcini flavour.

Transfer to a serving plate and season with salt and pepper.

Arcimboldo di Vittorio

Vittorio's Arcimboldo-Style Vegetables

Serves 8

50 ml good-quality virgin
olive oil

1 eggplant (aubergine),
roughly cut into
large pieces

3–4 onions, quartered

a piece of pumpkin

2 capsicums (peppers),
quartered (not deseeded)

3–4 zucchini (courgettes),
larger ones cut in half

3–4 ripe red tomatoes and
2 green tomatoes, halved –
or quartered if large

3 celery stalks

4–5 cloves garlic

2–3 mild, long chillies

1 bunch fresh basil
or oregano

salt

My friend Vittorio, the creator of this dish, says it is 'obligatory'
to use a heavy copper saucepan when making it so the vegetables
keep their vibrant colour. Ideally the ingredients should come
straight from your own garden.

Put the olive oil in the bottom of your copper pan. Now add the
vegetables, first the hard ones (eggplant, onions, pumpkin) then
the capsicum, zucchini and tomatoes, and finally the celery,
garlic, chillies and herbs. Season to taste with salt.

Put the pan on low heat with the lid on and let it cook gently
for about 1 hour. From time to time gently shake the pan, so
the vegetables won't stick to the bottom, but do not stir. Remove
from the heat and allow to cool to room temperature – about
15 minutes.

Variation

You can add a few anchovies, in which case be careful when adding
salt. Serve with either some boiled rice or some tajerini (page 221),
or just some crunchy bread. It is delicious as a lunch dish.

Note

If you have a vegetable garden, you can use virtually any
vegetable that is in season.

Peperoni alla Piemontese

Capsicums Piemontese-Style

Serves 4–6

5 very ripe medium
  tomatoes

4 red capsicums (peppers)

1 yellow capsicum (pepper)

20 anchovy fillets

4 cloves garlic, very
  thinly sliced

1 handful fresh oregano
  leaves

50 ml good-quality virgin
  olive oil

salt and ground black
  pepper

Preheat the oven to 180°C (gas mark 4).

Immerse the tomatoes for 1 minute in boiling water in order to loosen the skin, peel then cut them in half.

Char the capsicum skins, holding them over a flame (a gas burner or kitchen blow torch) with a pair of tongs, turning them all over until blackened. Then place them, still hot, in a plastic bag and leave for 5–10 minutes. (The steam will loosen the skin of the capsicums and make them very easy to peel.)

Cut the capsicums in half, making sure you also cut the stem in half (this is for visual effect). Remove the seeds and any filaments. Into each half put 2 anchovy fillets, a little sliced garlic and some oregano, then put a half tomato on top of the anchovy. Sprinkle over the olive oil and season (be careful when adding salt as the anchovies are already salty).

Bake in the oven for about 30 minutes.

You can serve these peperoni as an appetiser, as part of an antipasto or as an accompaniment to grilled veal, pork or beef. The peperoni also taste delicious when eaten cold.

Peperoni Farciti

Stuffed Capsicums

Serves 8

4–5 red capsicums (peppers)

16–20 anchovy fillets

16–20 fresh basil leaves

PÂTÉ DI TONNO

150 g unsalted butter

1 large Spanish onion,
chopped

1 large shallot, peeled
and chopped

2 sprigs fresh tarragon,
chopped

10 anchovy fillets, chopped

125 ml oloroso sherry

400 g canned tuna in oil

pepper

Char the capsicum skins, holding them over a flame (a gas burner or kitchen blow torch) with a pair of tongs, turning them all over until blackened. Then place them, still hot, in a plastic bag and leave for 5–10 minutes. (The steam will loosen the skin of the capsicums and make them very easy to peel.) Peel and deseed, then dry the capsicum with kitchen paper and set aside.

For the pâté, use about 50 g of the butter to cook the onion and shallot in a frying pan. Add the tarragon and anchovies and cook gently until the anchovies melt. Add the sherry and let it evaporate a little. Add the remaining butter and let it melt, but not cook.

Place the drained tuna in a food processor and add the butter and onion mix. Process until it becomes light in colour and add pepper.

Cut the capsicums lengthways into 2 cm slices, and on each slice put an anchovy fillet, a basil leaf and a heaped tablespoon of the pâté di tonno. Roll the capsicum slices, making neat little bundles and secure them with a toothpick.

Arrange on a serving plate and serve as an antipasto by themselves, or as part of a larger antipasto platter.

Variation

You can also use baby capsicums (pictured). Char the skin and remove as described above, but do not slice. Remove the tops and discard the seeds, then stuff the whole capsicum with pâté di tonno.

Peperonata Siciliana

Sicilian Capsicums

Serves 6

3 large red capsicums
(peppers)

3 large yellow capsicums
(peppers)

1 large green capsicum
(pepper)

TOPPING

50 g black olives, pitted

10 anchovy fillets in oil,
drained

140 g capers in brine,
drained

40 g pine nuts

3 cloves garlic

1 handful fresh mint leaves

125–200 ml good-quality
virgin olive oil

1 small red chilli

The Italians have a saying: 'First you eat with your eyes'. When you see this dish with its vibrant colours you can see why they say this.

Char the capsicum skins, holding them over a flame (a gas burner or kitchen blow torch) with a pair of tongs, turning them all over until blackened. Then place them, still hot, in a plastic bag and leave for 5–10 minutes. (The steam will loosen the skin of the capsicums and make them very easy to peel.) Peel and deseed, then cut each capsicum into 4–6 slices. Pat them dry with kitchen paper and arrange them on a serving platter.

To make the sauce, simply put all the ingredients in a blender and process until just amalgamated. Be careful not to over-blend – you should still see the individual ingredients. Spoon some of the sauce over the capsicums and serve the rest on the side in a little bowl.

This dish should be eaten at room temperature.

Porri e Patate al Forno

Leek and Potato Gratin

Serves 6

50 g unsalted butter

3 tablespoons good-quality
virgin olive oil

6 young leeks, trimmed
and sliced

3 cloves garlic, thinly sliced

1 kg waxy potatoes, such as
Desiree or King Edward,
very thinly sliced

350 ml cream

2 sprigs fresh rosemary,
stalks discarded

salt and ground black
pepper

The sweetness of the leeks infuses the potatoes to make this dish something special. You can serve it as an accompaniment to meat or even fish.

Preheat the oven to 200°C (gas mark 6).

Heat the butter and oil in a large saucepan. Add the leeks and garlic, cover the pan and sweat over a low heat for 15 minutes, stirring from time to time. The leeks should be soft and sweet.

Butter an ovenproof dish and arrange a layer of sliced potatoes over the base. Cover with some of the leeks, then pour on some cream and sprinkle with some of the rosemary and salt and pepper. Continue layering until all the ingredients are used up. Finish with a layer of potatoes, covered with cream, and sprinkled with rosemary, salt and pepper.

Transfer the potatoes to the oven and bake for around 35 minutes until the top is golden-brown.

Scaloppine alla Valdostana

Valdostana Veal

Serves 4

about 8 veal scaloppine,
2 per person (depending
on the size of the
scaloppine)

250 g fontina cheese,
sliced thinly

24 fresh sage leaves

unbleached plain flour,
for dusting

50 g unsalted butter

4 tablespoons good-quality
virgin olive oil

4 cloves garlic, crushed

150 ml dry white wine

salt and ground black
pepper

Flatten the scaloppine by beating them with a meat tenderiser.
Put a slice of fontina cheese on each scaloppine and fold the
meat over. Secure the scaloppine with a toothpick and thread a
fresh sage leaf through the toothpick. Now dust the scaloppine
with flour.

Melt the butter with the olive oil, add the garlic and the rest
of the sage leaves, then the veal. Fry the scaloppine on all sides,
until golden. Now add the dry white wine and continue cooking,
turning the scaloppine a few times, until cooked – about
5 minutes. Add salt and pepper to taste. If the sauce looks dry,
add a little stock.

Serve immediately while still hot. I like to serve this with
Patate Arrosto con Funghi Porcini (page 226).

Sottilina

Thin Scaloppine

Serves 4

4 veal scaloppine

plain flour, for dusting

1 organic egg, beaten

50 g breadcrumbs,
   for coating

50 g unsalted butter

80 ml good-quality virgin
   olive oil

1 handful fresh sage leaves

salt and ground black
   pepper

organic lemon wedges

I like to serve this dish with halved cherry tomatoes and some rocket scattered over the top for both taste and colour.

Get your butcher to cut the scaloppine quite thick and then, with a meat tenderiser, flatten them into a round shape, as big as a plate. Dust the surface of the meat with a little flour, coat with some beaten egg, then press the meat into the breadcrumbs.

Melt the butter in a frying pan and add the oil and sage leaves. When the butter foams, cook the scaloppine well on both sides until golden. Season with salt and pepper, and serve with a few wedges of lemon, or add some rocket and cherry tomatoes.

Rotolo di Vitello

Rolled Veal

Serves 4

large slice of top round
of veal (see Method)

salt and ground black
pepper

100 g prosciutto, thinly
sliced

2 veal kidneys, skin and
fat removed

20 fresh sage leaves

30 g unsalted butter

25 ml good-quality virgin
olive oil

2–3 cloves garlic, crushed

375 ml good-quality dry
white wine

stock, for moisture, if
needed

Get the butcher to cut a large piece of the top round of veal, cut across the grain (so that it does not shrink during cooking) and about 2 cm thick. This is the cut one uses to make scaloppine, but for this recipe you need a slice from the thicker part of the muscle. Pound the veal out nice and thinly – it should be as rectangular as possible!

Lay the veal flat and season it with salt and pepper. Put the prosciutto in a layer covering the meat, then put the whole veal kidneys side by side in the middle of the piece of meat with 10 sage leaves over the top. Now roll the meat very tightly and secure with a string that you knot every 5 cm along the roll.

Melt the butter and oil in a frying pan that is large enough to hold the veal roll comfortably. Brown the meat all over. Add the garlic and the remaining sage leaves, then pour the wine over the veal, turning it around several times. Put a lid on the pan, turn the heat down to low and cook the rotolo, basting and turning it from time to time, for about 1–1½ hours, depending on the thickness of the roll. If the meat looks too dry add a little stock to the pan.

Remove from the oven and let the meat rest for a few minutes, then carve it into slices about 1 cm thick. Pour the meat juices over the veal and serve.

Ucelli Scappati

Flown-away Birds

Serves 6

300 g calf's liver, sliced about 2 cm thick

300 g veal nut (noix, or topside), sliced about 2 cm thick

150 g pancetta, sliced 5 mm thick

unbleached plain flour, for dusting

fresh sage leaves

25 g unsalted butter

25 ml good-quality virgin olive oil

2–3 cloves garlic, chopped

300 ml dry white wine

salt and ground black pepper

chicken or veal stock for moisture, if needed

They are called 'ucelli scappati' (which means 'flown-away birds') because the combination of the pancetta, veal and liver apparently tastes like the wild birds that were once used.

Cut the liver, veal and pancetta into square cubes. Dust the liver and veal with flour. Then, alternating, thread the liver, sage, veal and pancetta on skewers.

Take a pan large enough to hold all the skewers at once and, in the butter and oil, brown the skewers of meat one or two at a time on all sides, then set aside in a dish.

Add the garlic to the pan with a few more sage leaves. Let the garlic become golden (do not burn it) then add the wine and scrape up all the bits in the bottom of the pan. When it bubbles add the skewers, salt and pepper and let them cook, covered and on low heat, for about 20 minutes.

If the dish seems too dry before cooking is finished, add a bit of veal or chicken stock.

Bonèt

Maria Teresa's Bonèt

Serves 8

200 g caster sugar

2 tablespoons water

5 fresh organic eggs

100 g Lindt or good-quality
  white chocolate

750 ml hot milk

75 g good-quality Italian
  amaretti biscuits (these
  should be small and a little
  bitter), finely crumbled

pinch of salt

40 ml Nocino liqueur
  (see Note) or rum

Preheat the oven to 180°C (gas mark 4).

In a saucepan, boil 125 g of the caster sugar and the water until the syrup is golden-brown and has caramelised. Pour the caramel into a large mould or individual moulds, covering the bottom evenly by tipping the dishes around in a circular motion. Set aside.

Beat the eggs and remaining sugar with an electric beater until light and fluffy. Dissolve the chocolate in the hot milk, and add this, beating constantly, to the egg mixture. Add the amaretti crumbs and salt, and finally add the liqueur.

Place the mould(s) in a large baking dish and fill with enough hot water to come a third of the way up their sides. Place in the oven and bake for 1 hour for one large mould, or 25 minutes for individual moulds.

Remove from the oven and let the bonèt cool in the mould(s), then slide a sharp knife all around the inside of the mould(s) and turn upside down onto a serving dish.

Serve with some whipped cream with a bit of Nocino or rum in it.

Note

Nocino is a traditional Italian liqueur made with walnuts. With this recipe you can make one bonèt in a single large mould, or eight smaller ones in individual moulds.

Traditionally, bonèt is made with cocoa powder.

Baci della Mamma

Mother's Kisses

Makes about 45 biscuits

250 g unsalted butter,
  at room temperature

60 g caster sugar

300 g unbleached plain flour

140 g hazelnuts, toasted and
  skin removed, as described
  on page 255, then roughly
  pounded

1–2 teaspoons salt

50 g icing sugar, for coating

Preheat the oven to 200°C (gas mark 6).

In a mixer beat the butter and sugar together until light in colour and fluffy. Add the flour, hazelnuts and salt, and mix for a short time until the dough is just amalgamated.

Put some greaseproof paper on an oven tray. Take a little of the dough and between your hands roll it into little oval balls, about 2 cm in diameter. Lay the balls out, side by side, on the tray, and bake in the oven until they are lightly golden, about 10–15 minutes.

Take the tray out of the oven, allow the biscuits to cool slightly before touching them (otherwise they will break apart) and then let them cool on a wire rack.

In a large bowl sift the icing sugar and then gently roll the little biscuits in it, until well coated.

Semifreddo alla Nocciola

Hazelnut Semifreddo

Serves 6

250 g caster sugar

300 g hazelnuts, toasted and
skin removed, as described
on page 255

2 organic eggs, separated

600 ml thickened cream

2 tablespoons Nocino
liqueur or oloroso sherry

melted dark chocolate, to
serve (optional)

To make the praline, melt 200 g of the sugar in a saucepan over medium heat, until golden-brown, tipping the pan from side to side so that the sugar will melt evenly. Stir in the hazelnuts and shake them around, until the caramelised sugar has coated them evenly. Pour onto some greaseproof paper and, with the back of a spoon, smooth the mix out to spread the nuts evenly (be careful, the praline will be very hot!).

When cold, break off pieces and pulse them in a food processor. The praline should not be too finely chopped: it should still be recognisable as little bits of hazelnut and caramel.

Beat the egg yolks with the remaining 50 g sugar, until light and fluffy, then add the cream slowly to the yolk mixture and beat for a few minutes more, adding the Nocino or sherry at the end. The mixture should have the consistency of a thick cream. Add the praline mixture and with a spoon fold it in well.

In a separate bowl, beat the egg whites until they form stiff peaks but are not dry. Fold into the praline mixture. Spoon the mixture into a rectangular dish. Cover with plastic wrap and freeze for at least 4 hours, or overnight.

Before serving, drizzle with melted dark chocolate, if desired.

Note

You can make the semifreddo in individual dishes if you prefer.

Torta alle Nocciole e Cioccolato Amaro

Hazelnut and Bitter Chocolate Cake

Serves about 10

400 g hazelnuts

400 g dark chocolate (70% cocoa solids)

400 g unsalted butter, at room temperature

300 g caster sugar

pinch of salt

10 organic eggs

Preheat the oven to 160°C (gas mark 3).

Place the hazelnuts in a dry frying pan and roast them over gentle heat until they are just starting to take a bit of colour, but do not burn them. Put them in a clean tea towel, fold the towel over and with your hands rub the nuts backwards and forwards; this movement will remove the skin.

Put the nuts in a food processor and pulse until they are ground finely but not to a paste.

Place the chocolate in a saucepan over hot water and, without stirring, let it melt. Remove from the heat and cool slightly.

Using an electric mixer, beat the soft butter with the sugar, adding the pinch of salt. When the mixture is light and fluffy, add the melted chocolate, blending well. Still blending, add one egg at a time, until well incorporated. Now fold in the crushed hazelnuts with a spatula.

Pour the mixture into a buttered cake tin, 28 cm in diameter, and bake in the oven for about 40 minutes, or until a skewer inserted in the cake comes out clean. Open the oven door and turn off the heat, leaving the cake in for another 30 minutes.

Tronchetto

Chocolate and Nougat Roll

Serves 10

4 organic egg yolks

175 g caster sugar

175 g unsalted butter,
  at room temperature

100 g good-quality
  cocoa powder

pinch of salt

200 g torrone (nougat),
  cut into largish pieces

150 g savoiardi (sponge
  finger) biscuits

200 g hazelnuts, toasted
  and skin removed, as
  described on page 255,
  then roughly pounded

Beat the egg yolks and sugar together, then add the butter and finally the cocoa powder and salt.

In a food processor, break up the torrone and savoiardi. Make sure you do not pulverise them, but leave them in quite largish chunks. Add them to the egg mixture with the hazelnuts and mix well.

On a long piece of aluminium foil, pour the mixture into a sausage shape and, with your hands, press it into a tight mass. Cover it with the foil and roll the sausage so that it becomes even. Leave it in the refrigerator for at least 3 hours.

Slice the tronchetto into 1 cm thick discs and serve with coffee.

Dolce di San Giuseppe

Monica's St Joseph's Dessert

Serves 8

25 savoiardi (sponge finger)
  biscuits

250 ml dry Marsala

350 g unsalted butter,
  at room temperature

3 fresh organic eggs,
  separated

175 g caster sugar

250 g hazelnuts, toasted
  and skin removed, as
  described on page 255,
  then finely ground

125 ml very strong
  espresso coffee

pinch of salt

few drops pure
  vanilla essence

200 g dark chocolate
  (70% cocoa solids;
  optional)

Use a high-sided mould, about 10 cm high and 18 cm wide. Take a piece of cheesecloth (muslin) that will easily line the mould, wet it then squeeze out absolutely all the water and line the mould with it.

Dip the biscuits into the Marsala, squeeze them so they flatten, and line the bottom and sides of the mould completely with the biscuits, pressing them well into the surfaces.

With an electric mixer, beat the butter until it becomes very fluffy; set aside.

Now beat the egg yolks and sugar together until pale yellow and fluffy. Add the hazelnuts, coffee, salt and vanilla. With a spatula mix the butter and egg–hazelnut mixture together until well amalgamated.

Beat the egg whites until stiff but not dry, and gently fold into the rest of the cake.

Put the mixture into the mould, pressing it down well. Cover with plastic wrap and refrigerate for at least 6 hours or, better still, overnight.

Carefully remove the cake from the mould, turn it over onto a serving plate and unwrap it. Melt the dark chocolate and pour it over the cake, if desired.

Torta di Noci

Walnut Cake

Serves 8

180 g fresh breadcrumbs

200 g walnuts, lightly
toasted

300 g caster sugar

100 g unsalted butter,
at room temperature

6 organic eggs, separated

200 g fresh ricotta

1 teaspoon ground
cinnamon

½ teaspoon ground cloves

grated zest of 1 organic
lemon

pinch of salt

1 tablespoon icing sugar,
for dusting

*This cake uses breadcrumbs and ground walnuts instead of flour.
It is a very light but fragrant cake, ideally eaten with afternoon tea.*

Preheat the oven to 190°C (gas mark 5).

Butter the sides of a 23 cm cake tin and line the base with
greaseproof paper. Sprinkle 15 g of the breadcrumbs onto the
sides of the cake tin, pressing them in gently.

Combine the walnuts with half the sugar in a food processor
and pulse until you have a fine, flour-like consistency.

In an electric mixer, beat the rest of the sugar with the butter
until very light and fluffy. Add the egg yolks, one at a time, and
continue beating until they are all incorporated and the mixture
is light and airy. Fold in the ground walnut mixture, ricotta,
remaining breadcrumbs, spices, lemon zest and salt.

In a separate bowl, whisk the egg whites to stiff peaks. Fold
into the cake batter then pour into the cake tin. Transfer to the
oven and bake for 35–40 minutes.

Remove from the oven, release the sides of the tin and remove
the cake. Leave to cool completely then place the cake on a
serving plate and dust with icing sugar.

Torta al Bianco D'uovo

Egg White Cake

Serves 6

125 g unsalted butter, plus extra for greasing

8 organic egg whites

200 g caster sugar

1 teaspoon pure vanilla extract

pinch of salt

125 g unbleached self-raising flour

100 g slivered almonds

1 teaspoon ground cinnamon

This is my father's favourite cake. I find that I always end up with extra egg whites in the fridge, so this is an ideal way of using them.

Preheat the oven to 180°C (gas mark 4) and butter a 25 cm springform cake tin.

Melt the 125 g butter and leave it to cool a little.

Beat the egg whites until they start to hold peaks then, while still beating, slowly add the sugar, reserving about 1 tablespoon for dusting, until the mixture becomes shiny. Add the vanilla and salt to the melted butter. Fold a little of the butter into the egg whites, then fold in some of the flour. Continue until all the butter and flour have been added. Pour the mixture into the tin.

Combine the almonds, cinnamon and the extra sugar. Sprinkle this evenly over the cake mixture.

Bake the cake in the oven for about 40 minutes, or until it springs back a little when touched. Cool the cake on a rack before serving.

Inverno

WINTER

Winter

Italian winter cooking is unusual because it has a strong seasonal character but few fresh ingredients. Most plants are dormant at this time so traditionally the only fresh ingredients have been from farm animals – eggs, milk, cheese and meat. Most of the traditional winter dishes use foods collected in summer or autumn and stored for the winter, so you draw on your supply of hams, salamis, cheeses, grains and pulses. In the cellar, potatoes, cabbages, onions, carrots and other root vegetables are stored, along with apples, nuts and raisins.

The more extreme your local climate, the more restricted your diet. The villages at the head of the Val Sesia in Piemonte are so high, and their summer so limited, that the local diet is little more than variations of bread (for which I have included a recipe) and cheese. Another recipe, Zuppa Valdostana, uses the same bread softened in broth.

Down in the valleys, food choices are more abundant and varied. It's the time for heavier pasta dishes – pappardelle, macaroni, pizzoccheri and spaezle. Polenta has always been a staple in the foothills around Lugano, with corn cobs stored in the airy attics of local houses.

Meat is a more important part of the diet – game if you can get it, and lamb or veal. Also in midwinter there is the traditional Christmas festive season with all the special occasion foods that go with it. In our family that means turkey, pâtés and a spectacular chestnut and cream dessert, Monte Bianco.

All in all there is a strong seasonal character to winter foods born of necessity in earlier times. Now we look forward to some of these heavier, slow-cooked dishes that suit the season and bring their own associations and pleasures.

Birebrot

Pear Bread

Makes a loaf of about 1 kg

DOUGH

300 g unbleached plain flour

4 teaspoons caster sugar

1 tablespoon dry yeast

½ teaspoon salt

50 g unsalted butter

150 ml warm milk

FILLING

250 g dried pears, soaked
   overnight in 100 ml merlot

60 g each dried figs, pitted
   prunes and pitted dates

50 g each currants,
   sultanas, almonds,
   hazelnuts and walnuts

50 g brown sugar

2 teaspoons ground
   cinnamon

1 teaspoon each ground
   cloves, ground cardamom
   and ground coriander

½ teaspoon ground nutmeg

grated zest of 1 organic
   lemon

100 ml Nocino liqueur
   or kirsch

50 ml rosewater

EGG WASH

1 organic egg yolk

1 tablespoon milk or cream

This is a very traditional bread with a sweet fruit filling. We eat it for breakfast, as a snack during the day or after dinner with some cheese and fresh pears. Spread it with a little butter or, as the Swiss like to eat it, with cheese.

Place all the dough ingredients in a food processor and process using a dough hook for 5–10 minutes, until the dough is shiny and slightly elastic (when you press a finger into the dough, the impression should spring back slowly). You may need to add a little more milk if the dough seems too dry or more flour if too wet. Transfer the dough to a bowl, cover with a cloth and leave in a warm place for about 1 hour, or until it has doubled in size.

Preheat the oven to 200°C (gas mark 6).

Place all the filling ingredients in a food processor and mix until you get a thick mass, ideally with some small chunks of fruit and nuts remaining.

Knock the air out of the dough and knead it for a few minutes. Roll the dough out to a thin rectangle of about 30 × 40 cm. Put the filling in the centre of the dough and shape it into a thick sausage running along the length of the dough. Wrap the dough around the filling, making sure there are no gaps, and trim away any excess dough. Place the loaf on an oven tray lined with greaseproof paper.

Combine the egg wash ingredients and brush over the loaf. Pierce holes all over the loaf with a fork. With the left-over dough you can make small decorations to go on top of the birebrot.

Bake the bread in the oven for about 20 minutes, or until the crust is golden-brown.

Pane Vallesano con Noci

Walser Nut Bread

Makes a loaf of about 1 kg

SOURDOUGH STARTER

150 g rye flour

200 ml warm water

1 tablespoon natural
 yoghurt (with acidophilus)

BREAD

2 tablespoons dry yeast

1 tablespoon honey

100 ml warm water

200 g wholemeal spelt flour

200 g rye flour

150 g whole rye grains,
 soaked in water
 overnight, drained

100 g walnuts, broken
 into pieces

2 teaspoons salt

This is a fabulous dark bread that keeps fresh for several days. The sourdough starter gives the bread a strong flavour and it needs to be made two or three days in advance. For a quicker bread, you can make this without the starter – it is still delicious. Just increase the rye flour to 350 g. When making bread, I use organic flour and grains wherever possible.

Combine the starter ingredients in a bowl and cover with a cloth. Leave in a warm place for 2–3 days, stirring from time to time, until it starts to froth.

To begin the bread, combine the yeast, honey, warm water and 1 tablespoon of spelt flour in a large mixing bowl. Leave for a few minutes, until the mixture begins to bubble. Add the sourdough starter, the remaining spelt flour, rye flour, soaked grains, walnuts and salt and mix to combine. If the mixture seems a little dry, add more water, or if too wet, add some extra spelt flour.

Turn the mixture onto a work surface and knead for 5–10 minutes until the dough is shiny and slightly elastic (when you press a finger into the dough, the impression should spring back slowly).

Form the dough into a ball, put it back into the mixing bowl and cover with a cloth. Leave it to rise in a warm spot for about 1 hour.

Knock the air out of the dough and form it into a long, wide loaf. Place on a baking tray and let it rise for another hour.

Preheat the oven to 200°C (gas mark 6).

Bake the bread for 20–25 minutes. To test if it is done, tap on the underside; it should sound hollow. Cool the bread on a rack.

Muesli di Michele

Michele's Muesli

500 g rolled oats

500 g rolled triticale

500 g rice bran or bran mixture

250 g ground almonds

250 g pepitas

250 g sunflower seeds

250 g linseeds

250 g unhulled sesame seeds

250 g lecithin granules

250 g shredded coconut

300 g sultanas

The nice thing about making your own muesli is that, by changing some of the ingredients, you can be creative and 'design' your own personal muesli. This is the muesli that I make for my husband, Michele.

I prepare this muesli in fairly large quantities. To keep it absolutely fresh (and this does make a difference) I store it in large glass jars in the freezer. This stops the grains from becoming stale and the nuts rancid, and keeps it crunchy. Michele eats it straight out of the freezer mixed with sheep's yoghurt and manuka honey (which is said to have healing properties).

Combine all the ingredients and store in the freezer.

Minestra D'orzo alla Grigionese

Pearl Barley Soup

Serves 4–6

20 g unsalted butter

2 tablespoons good-quality virgin olive oil

1 onion, finely chopped

1 leek, washed well and finely chopped

2–3 medium carrots, finely diced

1–2 stalks celery, finely diced

½ small celeriac, peeled and finely diced

1 fresh bay leaf

150 g smoked speck or bacon, diced

2 litres good-quality chicken or vegetable stock

100 g pearl barley

2 medium potatoes, peeled and diced

sea salt and ground black pepper

200 ml cream

This is a very hearty soup, ideal for a warming lunch after a long morning's skiing or working outdoors.

Heat the butter and oil in a saucepan. Add the onion and leek and cook gently for about 10 minutes. Now add the carrots, celery, celeriac, bay leaf and speck or bacon and turn the heat to medium. Cook for 10 more minutes, stirring from time to time. Add the stock, barley and potatoes and simmer gently for about 1 hour. Taste for salt and pepper and season.

Remove from the heat, add the cream and serve.

Zuppa Pavese

Pavese Soup

Serves 6

2.5 litres good-quality chicken stock

sea salt flakes

6 slices ciabatta bread

100 g grated Gruyère

100 g freshly grated parmigiano

6 organic eggs

1 bunch flat-leaf parsley, chopped

ground black pepper

There is a nice story about the origin of this soup. Cesare Pavese, a famous Italian poet, was walking in the mountains when a big storm surprised him and he had to seek shelter in a small mountain hut. The farmer was very honoured when he discovered who his guest was. As he had only bread and eggs to offer Pavese, he created this soup and named it after the great poet.

Put six wide soup bowls in a gentle oven just to heat them up (so the soup will stay piping hot).

Bring the chicken stock to a simmer and season. Keep the stock at simmering point while you grill or toast the ciabatta slices.

After toasting, place each slice of bread into a hot bowl. Combine the cheeses and sprinkle them over the bread. Pour the hot stock into the bowls and carefully break an egg on top of each slice of bread. Sprinkle some parsley and grind some pepper over the eggs. The heat of the stock should just cook the whites of the eggs, leaving the yolks deliciously runny.

Zuppa di Verdura della Evi

Evi's Vegetable Soup

Serves 6–8

25 g unsalted butter

2 tablespoons good-quality
   virgin olive oil

3–4 veal shanks, ends cut
   to expose the marrow

2 medium leeks, washed
   well, cut into small rounds

2 turnips, peeled and cut
   into small dice

1 small celeriac, peeled and
   cut into small dice

about 7 small carrots,
   cut into rounds

250 ml dry white wine

1 bunch cavolo nero (black
   cabbage), cut into strips

3 litres water

sea salt flakes and ground
   black pepper

1 bunch flat-leaf parsley,
   chopped

Heat the butter and oil in a large saucepan and brown the veal shanks on all sides. Transfer them to a plate and add the leeks to the pan. Cook the leeks over low heat for 10 minutes, until they become soft and sweet. Add the turnips, celeriac and carrots and cook, stirring, until they start to colour. Add the wine and stir well to deglaze the bottom of the pan. Let the wine evaporate over a medium heat. Add the cavolo nero, water, veal shanks and some salt and pepper to taste and let the soup simmer (covered with a lid) for about 1 hour, or until the meat is falling off the bones.

Remove the bones and, with a small spoon, scrape out the marrow. Stir the marrow into the soup. Break up any large chunks of meat in the soup with a wooden spoon.

Stir the parsley through the soup and serve with crusty bread.

Zuppa Valdostana

Valdostana Soup

Serves 6

2.5 litres good-quality
  chicken stock

unsalted butter,
  for greasing bowls

½ large Savoy cabbage

1 bunch cavolo nero
  (black cabbage)

¾ loaf ciabatta bread,
  thinly sliced and toasted

1 large clove garlic

20 anchovies in oil, drained

225 g fontina, roughly
  grated

225 g Gruyère, roughly
  grated

100 g freshly grated
  parmigiano

ground black pepper

This mountain soup is really a meal in itself, which is how it was traditionally served.

Preheat the oven to 200°C (gas mark 6).

In a large pan heat the chicken stock. Butter six large, ovenproof soup bowls.

Remove the leaves from the Savoy cabbage, cut away any thick stems and cut the leaves into large pieces. Cut the cavolo nero into large pieces.

Rub the toasted ciabatta bread with the garlic clove.

In the bottom of each bowl, put some cabbage and cavolo nero. On top of this place about 3 anchovy fillets then a handful of fontina and Gruyère cheeses. Arrange 1–2 slices of the toasted ciabatta on top. Continue with more layers of cabbage and cavolo nero, anchovies and parmigiano, then finally some ground pepper.

Now fill the bowls to three-quarters with the hot stock (do not fill them too full, as the bread will swell a bit during cooking). Cook them in the oven for about 15–20 minutes. The soup should have a nice golden, crunchy crust on top. Serve immediately.

Note

If you cannot find cavolo nero, substitute with fresh English spinach.

Nuvolone

Cloud Soufflé

Per person you will need:

2 organic eggs, separated

sea salt

50 ml cream

50 g grated Gruyère

ground black pepper

15 g unsalted butter

This dish is basically eggs in a party dress. It looks extraordinary as it arrives on the table, apparently the result of limitless time and skill. In fact it's fairly simple and takes no time at all – a winning combination to produce something that looks so good.

Serve it as a lunch dish with just a green salad and some crunchy bread.

Preheat the oven to 200°C (gas mark 6). Butter an individual ramekin per person (about 15 cm in diameter).

Beat the egg whites. When they start to become stiff, add salt to taste. Continue beating until they hold their peaks well.

Carefully drop the 2 egg yolks into the ramekin, then add the cream and Gruyère. Grind over some black pepper and add the butter. Spoon the egg whites over the cheese, cream and egg yolks.

Bake in the oven for 6–8 minutes. The top should be lightly golden, and when you break the crust, the yolks and cream should be soft and hot.

Serve with crusty bread to dip into the yolks and cream.

Soufflé di Formaggio

Cheese Soufflé

Serves 4

50 g unsalted butter

50 g unbleached plain flour

about 500 ml hot milk

200 g grated Gruyère

sea salt and ground black
pepper

4 organic eggs, separated

Preheat the oven to 180°C (gas mark 4). Butter a soufflé dish and put a collar of greaseproof paper around the rim of the dish.

Make a béchamel by melting the butter in a saucepan. Add the flour and stir well, letting it cook for a few minutes (be careful that it doesn't brown). Slowly add the hot milk, whisking vigorously so that no lumps form. When it has become the consistency of thick cream, turn off the heat and add the cheese, salt and pepper. Stir well until the cheese has melted. Add 1 egg yolk at a time to the sauce, mixing until well incorporated.

Beat the egg whites until they form peaks but are not dry. Gradually fold them through the béchamel, egg and cheese mixture. Pour the mixture into the soufflé dish and bake in the oven for about 40 minutes. It should be puffed up and golden-brown. Don't open the oven door to check on the soufflé while it's cooking or it will collapse (check through the glass instead). Serve immediately.

I like to serve the soufflé with a mixed salad.

Pizza Monica

Monica's Pizza

Serves 4

DOUGH

250 g potatoes

1 teaspoon dry yeast

200 ml warm milk

200 ml warm water

1½ teaspoons salt

400 g unbleached plain flour

TOMATO SAUCE

15 g unsalted butter

2 tablespoons good-quality
   virgin olive oil, plus extra
   for drizzling

1 small Spanish onion,
   finely chopped

1–2 cloves garlic, crushed

4 fresh sage leaves

1 sprig fresh rosemary

1 fresh bay leaf

75 g tomato paste

300 g canned peeled
   roma tomatoes

sea salt and ground black
   pepper

50 g grated Gruyère

50 g grated Emmental

For the dough, boil the potatoes in their skins until just done. Peel them and put them through a potato ricer, holding the ricer over a mixing bowl. Add the remaining dough ingredients to the bowl and mix well with a spoon. The dough should be shiny and quite wet, with a consistency similar to thick yoghurt.

Oil an oven tray (the best size to use is 30 × 20 cm, with a tall lip of about 5 cm around each side). Pour the dough into the tray and, with oiled hands, spread it to the edges. Let the dough stand in a warm place for 1 hour, or until it begins to rise and bubble.

Preheat the oven to 200°C (gas mark 6).

In the meantime, prepare the sauce. Heat the butter and oil in a saucepan and sauté the onion until softened, then add the garlic and herbs and cook for a further few minutes. Stir in the tomato paste and cook for a few minutes more, until it darkens in colour, but be careful not to burn it. Add the tomatoes, salt and pepper, put a lid on the pan and turn the heat down to low. Cook for about 15 minutes, stirring from time to time. Remove from the heat and discard the rosemary stalk and bay leaf.

Spread the tomato sauce over the pizza base and top with the cheeses. Drizzle a little olive oil on top and sprinkle with salt and pepper. Bake for about 20 minutes, or until the dough is cooked. The dough will rise quite high and the sauce will seep into it to create a soft pizza.

Torta di Cipolle

Onion Tart

Serves 4–6

PASTRY

15 g dry yeast

100 ml warm water

200 g unbleached plain flour

100 g unsalted butter,
  at room temperature

1 teaspoon salt

FILLING

50 g unsalted butter, plus
  extra for greasing

600 g onions, finely sliced

1 tablespoon good-quality
  virgin olive oil

150 g bacon, cut into strips

4 organic eggs

300 ml cream

100 g grated Gruyère

1 teaspoon sea salt

ground black pepper

For the pastry, combine the yeast and water and set aside.

Put the flour, butter and salt in a bowl and rub the butter into the flour with your fingertips. Add the yeast and water and mix until it forms a dough (if it seems too dry, you may need to add a little more water). Knead the dough until smooth and shiny. (Alternatively, you can make the dough in a food processor.) Let the dough rest for about 30 minutes (it should rise just a little).

Preheat the oven to 220°C (gas mark 7).

For the filling, heat the butter in a saucepan and cook the onions for about 10 minutes on medium heat, until soft and sweet. Transfer them to a plate.

Add the oil and bacon to the pan and cook until the bacon starts to become brown and crisp (be careful not to burn it). Drain on kitchen paper.

Butter an ovenproof pie dish (around 25–30 cm in diameter). Roll out the pastry and press it into the dish, trimming off any excess.

Beat the eggs and cream in a mixing bowl then add the cheese, salt, a grinding of pepper and the onions. Pour the mixture into the pastry base and scatter the bacon on top.

Cook on the bottom shelf of the oven for 30–40 minutes, or until golden-brown in colour.

Note

You can serve this onion tart with a salad for lunch, or as a starter before dinner. It can also be made without the cheese, which will make the tart a little lighter.

Pappardelle con Ragù di Anatra

Pappardelle with Duck Ragù

Serves 4–6

25 g unsalted butter

2 tablespoons good-quality virgin olive oil

2 free-range duck breasts, trimmed of excess fat and sliced

50 g pancetta, diced

1 Spanish onion, thinly sliced

2 cloves garlic, thinly sliced

1 carrot, finely diced

1 stalk celery, thinly sliced

1 fresh bay leaf

6 fresh sage leaves

250 ml red wine, such as pinot noir

140 g tomato paste

800 g canned peeled roma tomatoes

sea salt and ground black pepper

500 g pappardelle

freshly grated parmigiano, for serving

Heat the butter and oil in a saucepan and brown the duck pieces all over. Set aside on a plate.

To the same pan add the pancetta, onion, garlic, carrot, celery and herbs and cook for a few minutes, until they begin to colour. Add the duck pieces, with any juices that have pooled on the plate, and the wine. Stir well, scraping off anything sticking to the bottom of the pan. When the wine has evaporated, add the tomato paste. Cook for a few minutes, then stir in the tomatoes.

Put a lid on the pan and cook over low heat for about 45 minutes, stirring from time to time. The sauce should become thick and rich and the duck meat very tender. Taste for salt and pepper.

Bring a large pan of salted water to the boil. Cook the pappardelle until al dente. Drain the pasta and put it into a warm serving dish. Add the ragù and combine well. Serve immediately with parmigiano.

Macaroni delle Alpi

Mountain Macaroni

Serves 4

300 g penne or macaroni

125 g unsalted butter

1 large onion, sliced

150 g bacon, diced

200 ml cream

1 fresh bay leaf

ground black pepper

100 g grated Gruyère

100 g grated Emmental

300 g potatoes, boiled in
their skins then cut into
2 cm cubes

This is a typical dish of the 'cucina povera' (poor man's cooking) that is served in the mountains. The traditional way to serve it is with puréed apples as an accompaniment. It is an unusual combination of salty and sweet, but it somehow works – although I prefer to eat the dish plain.

Preheat the oven to 200°C (gas mark 6).

Boil the penne in plenty of salted water until half-cooked (about 3 or 4 minutes). Drain and place in a buttered ovenproof dish, dotting with 25 g of the butter so the pasta doesn't stick.

Sauté the onion in another 25 g of the butter until soft, then add the bacon and cook until the mixture starts to colour. Remove from the heat, then add the cream, bay leaf and a grinding of pepper. Return to the heat and gently simmer for a few more minutes. Discard the bay leaf.

Add the cream sauce, cheeses and potatoes to the penne and mix everything together. Dot small pieces of the remaining butter over the top of the pasta. Bake in the oven for about 15 minutes, or until it bubbles and starts to turn golden.

Spaezle di Gabi

Gabi's Spaezle

Serves 6

SPAEZLE

700 g unbleached plain flour

1½ teaspoons sea salt

½ teaspoon freshly
  grated nutmeg

6 organic eggs

150 ml water

2 tablespoons good-quality
  virgin olive oil

170 g unsalted butter

1 Spanish onion

50 g breadcrumbs

freshly grated parmigiano,
  for serving

ground black pepper

My sister-in-law is the spaezle queen, and she gave me this recipe. Spaezle are delicious eaten by themselves, or you can use them in dishes that would normally have pasta or mashed potatoes, or as an accompaniment to stews or even Arrosto di Cervo (roast venison, page 324). The consistency of spaezle is a little denser than that of pasta. You will need a spaezle press or a potato ricer to make them.

Put the spaezle ingredients in a large bowl. Beat the mixture with a wooden spoon until it is smooth and some air bubbles have formed. It will take about 10–15 minutes, so you will need a bit of elbow grease! Alternatively, use a food processor with a dough hook.

Let the dough rest for about 1 hour, beating it from time to time.

Bring a large pan of salted water to the boil. Put 2–3 tablespoons of the dough into a spaezle press or ricer, and over the water push the 'little worms' of dough through, cutting them off with a sharp knife. They should be about 4 cm long. As soon as they float to the surface of the water, they are cooked. Scoop them out with a slotted spoon into a heated dish. Dot the cooked spaezle with small pieces of the butter so they don't stick to each other, and keep them warm in a low oven while you continue cooking the rest.

In a frying pan, heat the oil and 25 g of the butter. Sauté the onion until softened. Add the rest of the butter and the breadcrumbs and cook for about 2 minutes, or until the breadcrumbs are starting to become crisp. Add the spaezle and cook for a further few minutes.

Serve topped with parmigiano and pepper.

Pizzoccheri

Buckwheat Pasta with Vegetables

Serves 6

PASTA

250 g buckwheat flour

150 g unbleached plain flour

1 teaspoon sea salt

3 large organic eggs

1 tablespoon good-quality
virgin olive oil

VEGETABLES

2 tablespoons good-quality
virgin olive oil

125 g unsalted butter

2 medium onions, sliced

2 cloves garlic, chopped

6–8 fresh sage leaves

1 bunch cavolo nero (black
cabbage), stems discarded,
leaves roughly chopped

200 g potatoes, boiled in
their skins then diced
into 2–3 cm cubes

200 g young green beans,
cut into 2 cm pieces

100 g freshly shelled peas

200 g baby spinach

100 g grated Gruyère

sea salt and ground black
pepper

100 g freshly grated
parmigiano

Pizzoccheri is a traditional buckwheat pasta eaten as a hearty main meal. This version is delicious, baked with vegetables and cheese. If you do not have the time to make your own pasta, you can find pizzoccheri in good Italian delicatessens.

Mix the pasta ingredients into a dough; if it seems dry, add a few drops of water. Divide the dough into 3 or 4 pieces. Pass 1 piece through your pasta machine on a wide setting, then fold it up in order to pass it through again. Continue doing so until the dough is of a uniform consistency and shiny. Repeat with the other pieces of dough. Set the pasta machine to a medium setting and put the pieces through again to make large, thin sheets.

Lay the sheets on a floured surface and cut them widthways with a sharp knife into strips about 2 cm thick.

Preheat the oven to 220°C (gas mark 7).

For the vegetables, heat the oil and 25 g of the butter in a saucepan and gently cook the onions until soft. Add the garlic, sage and cavolo nero and cook for a few more minutes. Remove from the heat and add the potatoes, beans, peas and spinach and gently mix together.

Butter a large ovenproof dish. Bring a large pan of salted water to the boil and cook the pizzoccheri for just 1 minute. Drain and put the pasta into the dish. Add the vegetables, Gruyère and some salt and pepper and gently mix everything together. Sprinkle the parmigiano on top, then evenly dot the remaining butter over the top of the parmigiano. Bake the pizzoccheri in the oven for about 20 minutes, or until the top turns golden.

Pasta e Fagioli

Pasta and Beans

Serves 4–6

60 ml good-quality virgin
  olive oil, plus extra
  for drizzling

150 g pancetta, diced

2 large Spanish onions,
  sliced

2–3 stalks celery, sliced

2–3 carrots, sliced

2–3 cloves garlic, chopped

1 chilli

5 fresh sage leaves

2 bay leaves

1 sprig rosemary

½ bunch flat-leaf parsley,
  roughly chopped

4–6 pork sausages
  (optional), chopped into
  2 cm lengths

1 glass dry red or white
  wine

500 ml fresh chicken
  or veal stock

250 g dried borlotti
  beans, soaked overnight,
  or 400 g fresh beans
  (no need to soak)

800 g peeled roma tomatoes

500 g short pasta, such
  as shells or penne

salt and ground black
  pepper

freshly grated parmigiano,
  for serving

In a large saucepan heat the oil and fry the pancetta, sliced onion, celery, carrot, garlic and whole chilli. Add the herbs. If using, add the sausages and cook for a few minutes until the sausages start to brown. Now add the wine, stirring vigorously until it evaporates. Add the stock, then the borlotti beans and tomatoes. Let it all cook for about 30–45 minutes, covered, or until the borlotti beans are very tender.

Now add the pasta to the beans and vegetables. If the dish looks dry at this point, add more stock or water (the finished dish should be quite moist, and the pasta will take up liquid). Cook until the pasta is al dente or for about 10–12 minutes, depending on what pasta you use. Taste for salt and pepper and season.

Serve with freshly grated parmigiano and a little good-quality virgin olive oil on the table for drizzling.

Polenta Ghiotta

Food Lover's Polenta

Serves 4–6

POLENTA

1.5 litres water

1½ teaspoons sea salt

300 g coarse polenta

MUSHROOMS

25 g unsalted butter

2 tablespoons good-quality
  virgin olive oil

1 Spanish onion, finely
  sliced

2 cloves garlic, finely sliced

6 anchovies

1 bunch flat-leaf parsley,
  chopped

200 g mixed mushrooms,
  finely chopped

15 g dried porcini
  mushrooms, soaked
  in a little water for
  15 minutes, drained
  and finely sliced

sea salt and ground black
  pepper

150 g unsalted butter

15 sage leaves

To cook the polenta, put the water and salt in a large saucepan and bring to the boil. Add the polenta in a steady stream, whisking constantly to avoid lumps. Turn the heat down to low and cook the polenta for about 45 minutes, stirring from time to time. When the polenta comes away from the sides of the pan, it is cooked.

In the meantime, prepare the mushrooms. Heat the butter and oil in a saucepan and cook the onion until it begins to soften, then add the garlic, anchovies and parsley and cook for a further few minutes. Add all the mushrooms and continue cooking until soft. Taste for salt (remembering that the anchovies will have added some already) and grind over some pepper.

Stir the mixture into the cooked polenta, combining well. Pour the polenta into a tray lined with greaseproof paper, spreading the polenta to about 1.5 cm thick. Leave to cool.

Cut the cooled polenta into small squares or rectangles. Heat some of the butter in a frying pan and add a few sage leaves. Fry a few polenta shapes at a time, browning them on both sides.

Transfer to a warm oven while you cook the rest, using more of the butter and sage as you go.

This polenta dish is delicious served as an antipasto to go with drinks, or as a starter.

Polenta Pasticciata

Polenta Baked with Cheese

Serves 6–8

POLENTA

2–2.5 litres water

2 teaspoons sea salt

500 g coarse polenta

unsalted butter, for greasing

150 g Gruyère, thinly sliced

150 g Gorgonzola dolce,
  thinly sliced

250 g mascarpone

ground black pepper

When I make polenta I always like to make more than I need. Then I can use the left-over polenta the next day to make something marvellous. This is one of those 'next-day' recipes, baked in the oven to produce a rich and warming dish traditional to the foothills of the Italian Alps. The recipe also includes the instructions for basic polenta, which you can serve with Tonno in Umido (page 310).

To cook the polenta, put the water and salt in a large saucepan and bring to the boil. Add the polenta in a steady stream, whisking constantly to avoid lumps. Turn the heat down to low and cook the polenta for about 45 minutes, stirring from time to time. When the polenta comes away from the sides of the pan, it is cooked and ready to be served. Pour the polenta onto a wooden board or into a tray lined with greaseproof paper and leave to cool.

Preheat the oven to 200°C (gas mark 6).

Butter an ovenproof dish. Slice the polenta into 1 cm thick slices. Layer the bottom of the dish with a third of the polenta, then top with the Gruyère. Add another layer of polenta, then the Gorgonzola dolce. Add the final layer of polenta and spread with the mascarpone. Grind some pepper on top and bake in the preheated oven for about 20 minutes, or until golden.

Tonno in Umido

Tuna Stew

Serves 6

50 g unsalted butter

2 tablespoons good-quality
    virgin olive oil

1 large Spanish onion,
    chopped

2–3 cloves garlic, chopped

3 medium carrots, chopped

3 stalks celery, chopped

1 bunch flat-leaf parsley,
    chopped

1 fresh bay leaf

5 fresh sage leaves

140 g tomato paste

12 anchovies

800 g canned peeled roma
    tomatoes, broken up
    with your fingers

850 g canned tuna in oil,
    drained

250 g freshly shelled peas

sea salt and ground black
    pepper

Heat the butter and oil in a large saucepan and sauté the onion until softened, then add the garlic, being careful not to let it brown. Add the carrots, celery and herbs and cook for a further few minutes.

Add the tomato paste and anchovies and cook over medium heat for about 5 minutes. Add the peeled tomatoes and turn the heat down to low. Put a lid on the pan and cook for 30 minutes, stirring from time to time.

Put the tuna in the pan, breaking it into bite-sized pieces with the spoon, and then add the peas. Cook until the peas are tender (about 10 minutes).

Taste the stew for salt and pepper, discard the bay leaf, and serve.

Note

This wintry dish is traditionally served with polenta, for soaking up the delicious juices (see page 309 for a basic polenta recipe). It is also great served with mashed potatoes.

Fondue

Hot Cheese Dip

Serves 4

1 clove garlic

300 ml dry white wine

200 g coarsely grated
Gruyère

200 g coarsely grated
Emmental

200 g vacherin cheese
(such as vacherin à
fondue, but not Vacherin
Mont d'Or; if you can't
find vacherin, increase
Gruyère and Emmental
to 300 g each)

50 ml kirsch

2 tablespoons cornflour
(optional, but it helps
bind the sauce)

freshly grated nutmeg

ground black pepper

loaf of Italian ciabatta bread,
cut into bite-sized pieces

1 organic egg (optional)

Traditional cheese fondue is a dish with fairly frugal beginnings. It was simply what people did with left-over cheese – they melted it in an earthenware pot over a fire and dipped pieces of bread in. With time, the dish became more refined, and kirsch and white wine were added.

Rub the fondue pan with the garlic. Add the wine and put the pan over low heat on the stove. Heat the wine until close to boiling.

Gradually add the cheeses, stirring constantly. When they have melted, add the kirsch (if you are using the cornflour, stir it into the kirsch beforehand). The fondue should have a creamy consistency. Add a little nutmeg and a grinding of pepper.

Put the fondue pan in the middle of the table over a flame to keep the liquid lightly bubbling. With a fork, each person should spear a piece of bread and dip it into the fondue.

At the end of the meal, leave a little bit of cheese in the bottom of the pot and break the egg into it. Scramble the egg and cheese together and serve it as a final taste. (This last step is optional but well worth trying.)

Pâté di Fegato della Mamma

Mamma's Liver Pâté

Serves 6–8

GELATINE

250 ml water

1 chicken stock cube

3 gelatine leaves

250 g unsalted butter,
  cut into cubes

1 Spanish onion,
  finely chopped

3 cloves garlic,
  finely chopped

5 rashers bacon,
  finely chopped

8 fresh sage leaves

1 sprig fresh rosemary

1 fresh bay leaf

500 g chicken livers,
  trimmed of little white
  nerves and bile, chopped

400 g calf's liver, chopped

150 ml cognac or vin santo

1 teaspoon sea salt

ground black pepper

Bring the water and stock cube to the boil. Soften the gelatine leaves in a little cold water then add them to the stock, stirring to dissolve them. Pour the stock into a 25 cm long terrine dish and leave to cool, then put it in the refrigerator to set. Once set, you can decorate the jelly with herbs, decoratively cut vegetables or gold leaf if you wish.

In a large frying pan heat about 20 g of the butter and lightly fry the onion, garlic, bacon and herbs. Add the liver and cook for about 5–10 minutes, by which time it should be cooked but still a little pink in the middle. Add the cognac or vin santo, salt and a few grindings of pepper, stirring well. Let the liquid come just to the boil then turn off the heat and add the rest of the butter, letting it melt into the mixture. Discard the rosemary stalk and bay leaf.

Put the mixture into a food processor and process until you have a light, smooth mass. Taste to see if more salt is needed or even a touch more cognac or vin santo.

Spoon the pâté into the terrine dish, being careful not to disturb any decoration you may have put on the gelatine. Cover with plastic wrap and refrigerate for at least 3 hours or overnight.

To serve, run a sharp knife around the rim of the pâté then stand the dish in a little hot water for a few seconds to loosen the jelly on the bottom. Invert the pâté onto a serving plate and serve with crusty Italian bread or toast.

Polpettone con Uova Sode

Meat Loaf with Hardboiled Eggs

Serves 6–8

25 g unsalted butter

2 tablespoons good-quality virgin olive oil, plus extra for brushing

1 large Spanish onion, finely chopped

2–3 cloves garlic, crushed

2 stalks celery, finely sliced

2 carrots, finely chopped

10 fresh sage leaves

1 sprig fresh rosemary

200 ml vin santo, or oloroso sherry

600 g minced veal

600 g minced pork

600 g minced beef

2½ teaspoons sea salt

ground black pepper

200 g white bread, crusts removed, soaked in a little milk

2–3 bay leaves

200 g very thinly sliced bacon to line the terrine dish

6 slices leg ham (medium thickness), cut into long strips

8 organic eggs (2 raw, 6 hardboiled and peeled)

Preheat the oven to 220°C (gas mark 7).

Heat the butter and oil in a saucepan and cook the onion, garlic, celery, carrots and herbs for a few minutes, until the vegetables begin to colour lightly. Add the vin santo or oloroso sherry and let it boil for 2 minutes, then remove from the heat.

Put the meats, salt and pepper in a large bowl and mix together, then add the vegetables. Squeeze the bread of excess milk and break it into the mixture. Add the 2 raw eggs. Combine everything really well (I find it easiest to use my hands).

Line a large rectangular terrine dish or loaf tin (about 35 cm long) with foil and brush it with oil. Put 2–3 bay leaves in the middle of the dish as decoration, then line the bacon side to side over the whole bottom and side of the terrine. Put a third of the mince mixture in the tin and press it down evenly. Lay half the ham slices on top, then add a little more mince on top of the ham. Arrange the hardboiled eggs in a line down the centre, then enough extra mince to cover the eggs. Layer the remaining ham on top and add the remaining mince. If any bacon remains, cover the terrine with it. Press the mixture down well.

Bake the loaf on the bottom shelf of the oven for 50 minutes; it should be lightly browned on top. Turn the polpettone onto a serving dish. It is delicious served hot or cold with crusty bread.

Pollastrelli

Roast Spatchcock

Serves 4

4 × 500–600 g spatchcocks

6 cloves garlic, crushed

4 sprigs fresh rosemary, stems discarded and leaves roughly chopped

sea salt and ground black pepper

50 ml good-quality virgin olive oil

200 g unsalted butter

This dish was traditionally made with baby roosters – known as 'mistkratzerli', which translates as 'dung-scratchers' – because female chickens were kept for egg-laying.

Preheat the oven to 200°C (gas mark 6).

Rub the birds inside and out with some of the garlic and rosemary, and with salt and pepper. Leave some of the garlic and rosemary for making a sauce.

Heat the oil and 50 g of the butter in a frying pan. When the foam from the butter subsides, brown the birds until they are nicely coloured on all sides.

Place the birds in an oven dish and bake for about 30 minutes, basting from time to time with the juices from the pan and with an extra 50 g of melted butter.

Remove the birds from the oven and let them rest for a few minutes. Melt the remaining butter in a saucepan and add the leftover garlic and rosemary. Cook for a few minutes, being careful that the garlic doesn't brown. Pour the sauce over the birds and serve.

Agnello con Crosta di Patate

Lamb Pie with Potato Crust

Serves 4

CRUST

500 g potatoes, boiled in
  their skins, peeled and
  mashed

1 organic egg

150 g unbleached plain flour

1 teaspoon sea salt

FILLING

800 g lamb fillets or
  backstraps (loins),
  cut into 2 cm pieces

2 tablespoons unbleached
  plain flour, for dusting

50 g unsalted butter

2 tablespoons virgin olive oil

1 large Spanish onion, sliced

2 cloves garlic, crushed

2 carrots, diced

3 stalks celery, diced

1 parsnip, diced

2 sprigs fresh rosemary

10 fresh sage leaves

200 g thickly sliced leg
  ham, cut into thin strips

350 ml red wine

sea salt and ground black
  pepper

EGG WASH

1 organic egg

2 tablespoons cream

Preheat the oven to 200°C (gas mark 6).

Mix the mashed potato, egg, flour and salt into a dough. Let the dough rest for about half an hour.

For the filling, toss the pieces of lamb in the flour. Heat the butter and oil in a large saucepan and, when the butter foams, add the lamb. Brown the meat all over then transfer it to a plate. Add the onion, garlic, carrot, celery, parsnip and herbs to the pan and cook for about 5 minutes, until they start to soften. Stir in the lamb and ham, then add the wine. Cook until the wine has evaporated. Remove from the heat and season with salt and pepper.

Butter an oval ovenproof dish. Fill the dish with the meat and vegetables.

Roll the dough out between two lightly floured pieces of greaseproof paper until it is about 2 cm thick. Cut the dough to the shape of the dish and place this 'lid' over the meat and vegetables, pressing down around the edges of the dough to seal it. Roll a long sausage from the excess dough and with a fork press it around the rim of the dish. If you have any dough left over, you can decorate the lid with leaf shapes.

For the egg wash, beat the egg and cream together and brush it over the dough. Bake the pie in the oven for about 30 minutes, or until the crust is golden-brown.

Arrosto di Cervo

Roast Venison

Serves 4

VENISON

8 juniper berries

2 fresh bay leaves

10 peppercorns

1 small chilli

600 g venison fillet

SAUCE

1 bottle good-quality
  red wine

50 ml balsamic vinegar

3 shallots, roughly chopped

3 cloves garlic, crushed
  with a knife

8 juniper berries

6 cloves

1 fresh bay leaf

2 tablespoons brown sugar

25 g unsalted butter

sea salt and ground black
  pepper

25 g unsalted butter

1 tablespoon good-quality
  virgin olive oil

coarse sea salt

I use venison fillet in this recipe as it is incredibly tender and quick to cook – allow 150 g per person. Because it has no fat, the meat should be cooked rare to medium–rare. I like to serve this roast with spaezle (page 299).

For the venison, crush the juniper berries, bay leaves, peppercorns and chilli in a mortar. Rub this mixture into the meat and let it stand at room temperature for about 1 hour.

Preheat the oven to 180°C (gas mark 4).

In the meantime, put the sauce ingredients except the butter, salt and pepper in a saucepan and bring to the boil. Simmer gently until reduced to about 200 ml. Strain the liquid through a sieve and return it to the pan. Add the butter and heat until it melts into the sauce. Taste for salt and pepper. Keep warm while you cook the venison.

Heat the butter and oil in a frying pan and, as soon as the butter begins to foam, put the venison into the pan and brown it quickly on all sides, sealing in the juices. Transfer the meat to an oven tray and roast for about 10 minutes (if your venison weighs more or less than 600 g, calculate the cooking time based on 15 minutes per kilogram for rare, and 20 minutes per kilogram for medium–rare). It is important to rest the meat for as long as you cooked it in the oven, loosely wrapped in foil to keep it warm.

Slice the meat, place it on a warmed serving plate and pour over some sauce, then sprinkle some coarse sea salt over it. Put the rest of the sauce in a bowl to serve on the side.

Spezzatino di Vitello alla Zurighese

Zurich-Style Veal

Serves 6

2–3 tablespoons unbleached plain flour, for dusting

1 kg veal backstrap (loin), sliced into 2 cm strips

50 g unsalted butter

2 tablespoons good-quality virgin olive oil

1 onion, very finely sliced

2 cloves garlic, finely sliced

about 15 fresh sage leaves, chopped

200 g Swiss brown mushrooms, thickly sliced

250 ml dry white wine

sea salt and ground black pepper

300 ml cream

This is a specialty of Zurich, and I think one of the most delicious dishes prepared at the Kronenhalle restaurant there. It is usually served with potato rösti.

Sprinkle the flour over the meat to coat well.

Heat half of both the butter and oil in a frying pan. As soon as the butter foams, add the meat and brown it very quickly on all sides. Set aside on a plate.

Add the rest of the butter and oil to the pan and sauté the onion, garlic and sage for a few minutes, then add the mushrooms. Stir well and, when the mushrooms start to soften, continue cooking for about 5 minutes longer.

Add the wine to deglaze the bottom of the pan, using a wooden spoon to scrape away any crust that has formed. Add the veal and cook, stirring, until the wine has evaporated. Turn the heat down to low and cook for another 10 minutes.

Season with salt and pepper and, at the last moment, add the cream, allow it to bubble for 2 minutes, then remove the pan from the heat and serve.

Tacchino con Castagne

Turkey with Chestnut Stuffing

Serves 6

STUFFING

14–16 whole chestnuts

25 g unsalted butter

150 g chicken or duck livers, roughly chopped

1 Spanish onion, finely sliced

2 carrots, diced

2 stalks celery, diced

7 slices white bread, crusts removed (dice 6 slices into small cubes)

10 fresh sage leaves

2 sprigs fresh rosemary, leaves only

sea salt and ground black pepper

TURKEY

1 organic turkey weighing about 3 kg, or larger if you want leftovers for the next day

good-quality virgin olive oil, for rubbing

sea salt

250 ml sunflower oil

1 bottle vin santo (or oloroso sherry)

Preheat the oven to 220°C (gas mark 7).

For the stuffing, make an incision in the flat side of the chestnuts and roast them in the oven for 15 minutes. Let them cool, then peel and cut them in half. They should still be a little raw in the middle.

Heat the butter in a frying pan and sauté the livers, onion, carrots and celery until the livers are cooked but still a little pink inside. Put into a bowl with the chestnuts, diced bread, herbs, salt and pepper.

Wash the turkey inside and out under running water, then dry it well (including the inside) with kitchen paper. Rub the bird with olive oil and sprinkle a little salt into the main cavity (the turkey has two cavities – the main cavity between the legs and a smaller neck cavity).

Put some stuffing into the neck cavity without packing it too tightly, as the stuffing will swell a little as it absorbs the juices of the bird. With a large needle and some strong thread or string, sew the neck skin to the body of the bird to close the neck cavity. Fill the main cavity with the rest of the stuffing. Put the extra slice of bread at the entrance of this cavity to keep this stuffing in place. Tie the bird's legs together with string. Put the turkey on a large, deep oven tray.

In a small saucepan, heat the sunflower oil to a high temperature, then carefully pour it all over the bird to sear and seal the skin. This will keep the bird moist.

Put the turkey in the oven. After 10 minutes turn the heat down to 180°C (gas mark 4). Cook for 35 minutes per kilogram of turkey, basting from time to time with plenty of vin santo. If the turkey seems to darken too quickly, cover the breasts with foil to prevent the turkey from burning. Before carving, let the bird rest for 15 minutes in a warm place covered with foil.

Verdure della Mamma

Mamma's Baked Vegetables

Serves 4

2 medium leeks, white, tender parts only, halved lengthways, rinsed well under running water

½ small Savoy cabbage, sliced

½ small cauliflower, broken into small florets

4 stems broccolini

1 small sweet potato, thinly sliced

300 ml cream

sea salt and ground black pepper

200 g freshly grated parmigiano

70 g unsalted butter

My mother used to make these vegetables often in winter. By changing the vegetables, it becomes a new dish every time, so the vegetables used here are simply one suggestion.

Preheat the oven to 200°C (gas mark 6).

Butter a large ovenproof dish (about 30 × 40 cm). Lay the vegetables in rows next to each other. Pour over the cream and sprinkle with salt, pepper and parmigiano. Break the butter into little pieces and dot it over the vegetables.

Bake in the oven for about 25 minutes, or until the vegetables are tender and golden on top.

Capuns

Sausage-Stuffed Cabbage Rolls

Serves 4

20 medium cavolo nero
(black cabbage) or
silverbeet leaves

1 Spanish onion,
finely chopped

25 g unsalted butter

150 g organic pork sausage
(or any sausage you prefer,
such as lamb, chicken or
beef), cut into small pieces

200 g unbleached plain flour

2 large organic eggs

70 ml milk

150 g ricotta (this is
optional, but the capuns
are lighter with it)

40 g freshly grated
parmigiano, plus extra
for serving

½ bunch flat-leaf parsley,
finely chopped

ground black pepper

150 ml cream

100 ml good-quality chicken
or vegetable stock

4–5 slices prosciutto
(optional)

This recipe traditionally calls for silverbeet. I prefer to make it with cavolo nero as the leaves are more delicate in taste and appearance, but use whichever leaf you prefer.

Cut the stalks off the cavolo nero or silverbeet leaves and blanch the leaves in salted water. Dry on kitchen paper. Sauté the onion in the butter until soft, then add the sausage and cook for 5 minutes.

Combine the flour, eggs, milk, ricotta (if using), parmigiano and parsley in a bowl to form a batter. Add the onion and sausage and a grinding of pepper.

Place 1 tablespoon of filling on each blanched leaf and roll the leaves up tightly, making little parcels. Make sure the stuffing is completely wrapped.

Put the cream and stock in a large frying pan and bring to a simmer. Arrange the capuns in the pan so they fit snugly side by side. Cover with a lid and cook gently for about 20 minutes. Alternatively, place the sauce and capuns in an ovenproof dish, cover with foil, and bake in a 180°C (gas mark 4) oven for 20 minutes.

Serve the capuns in soup bowls with some of the sauce spooned over the top and sprinkled with parmigiano. If using, cook some thin strips of prosciutto in a little butter until crisp and use this as an extra garnish.

Insalata Mista

Swiss-Style Mixed Salad

Serves 4

50 g or 1 large handful
  Nüsslisalat
  (lamb's lettuce/mâche)

6–8 radicchio leaves, sliced
  in thin strips

1–2 medium carrots, grated

⅓ small celeriac, peeled
  and grated

1 Lebanese cucumber,
  peeled and sliced

SAUCE

50 ml red-wine vinegar

150 ml good-quality
  virgin olive oil

½ teaspoon sea salt

4 tablespoons home-made
  mayonnaise (page 166)

There is nothing better than eating a colourful and delicious salad like this one in the middle of a long, grey winter. It is like a ray of sunshine.

Arrange the salad leaves and vegetables separately around a large plate.

Put the vinegar, oil, salt and mayonnaise in a glass jar with a lid and shake vigorously until creamy. Pour the dressing over the salad and serve at once.

Note

Use Nüsslisalat for this winter salad, as it only grows during this season. Alternatively, you can use baby spinach leaves.

Radicchio alla Griglia

Grilled Radicchio

Serves 4

2 young radicchio

good-quality virgin olive
  oil, for drizzling

salt flakes

ground black pepper

I love this simple way of eating radicchio. It is a slightly bitter leaf with wonderful colour. Grilled like this, with extra virgin olive oil and salt, it becomes something special. It is particularly good as an accompaniment to grilled meat or fish, but can also be part of an antipasto.

Preheat a barbecue or griddle plate to high.

Cut the radicchio into quarter wedges and drizzle with olive oil. Grill or barbecue for a few minutes until the radicchio just starts to colour. Transfer to a serving dish and drizzle with a little more oil. Sprinkle with salt and pepper and serve.

Torta di Cioccolato Tipo Truffe

Chocolate Truffle Cake

Serves 6

125 g good-quality dark
chocolate (70% cocoa
solids)

125 g unsalted butter

5 organic eggs, separated

250 g caster sugar

2 tablespoons unbleached
plain flour

pinch of salt

whipped cream, for serving

This is really a 'no-holds-barred' chocolate cake for true chocolate
lovers. It just melts in your mouth.

Preheat the oven to 150°C (gas mark 2) and butter a 25 cm
springform cake tin.

Melt the chocolate and butter in a bowl set over a saucepan
of simmering water.

In a mixing bowl beat the egg yolks and sugar until fluffy, then
add the flour, salt and the butter and chocolate mixture. Stir well.

Beat the egg whites until they hold their peaks, then gradually
fold them into the cake mixture.

Pour the mixture into the tin and bake in the oven for
35 minutes, or until a light crust has formed on top but the
centre is still soft. Immediately release the cake from the tin,
let it cool on a rack (it will collapse a little), then refrigerate
overnight. Serve with cream.

Note
This cake tastes best if you make it the day before serving it.

For a super-indulgent dessert, put a layer of chocolate mousse
(page 342) over the top of this truffle cake.

Mousse al Cioccolato

Chocolate Mousse

Serves 4

100 g good-quality dark
   chocolate (70% cocoa
   solids)

40 g unsalted butter

50 ml Nocino liqueur
   (see Note)

4 organic eggs, separated

1 tablespoon cocoa powder,
   for sprinkling

whipped cream, for serving

Melt the chocolate and butter (without stirring) in a bowl set
over a saucepan of simmering water. Remove from the heat and
stir in the Nocino followed by the egg yolks, combining well.

Beat the egg whites until stiff, then gradually fold them
through the chocolate mixture. Pour the mousse into individual
dishes and refrigerate overnight. Or, do as they do at the
Kronenhalle restaurant in Zürich and refrigerate the mousse
in a large bowl, bring the bowl to the table and spoon it onto
dessert plates. Sprinkle with cocoa powder, if you like. Serve
with whipped cream.

Note

This mousse is better if you make it the day before – somehow it
becomes even more chocolatey. Nocino is an Italian liqueur made
from walnuts and spices. You can use vin santo or oloroso sherry
if you prefer.

Biscotti di Natale

Christmas Biscuits

During this festive season, it is a tradition in my family to make special Christmas biscuits. There are many different varieties — some with chocolate, some with nuts, and others are plain butter biscuits. We cut some of them into various shapes — angels, stars and Christmas trees. Some we leave plain and others we decorate with icing. It is a ritual in which children love to get involved, cutting out the biscuits or decorating them (and sneaking a few pieces of dough or fingerfuls of icing sugar).

Spekulatius

Makes about 30 biscuits

250 g unsalted butter,
  at room temperature

500 g caster sugar

3 organic eggs

500 g unbleached plain flour

pinch of salt

2 teaspoons ground
  cinnamon

1 teaspoon ground cloves

grated zest of 1 organic
  lemon

Cream the butter and sugar until light and fluffy, then add 1 egg at a time, beating well after each addition. Add the remaining ingredients and mix thoroughly. Shape the dough into a ball and refrigerate for about 1 hour.

Preheat the oven to 180°C (gas mark 4).

Roll the pastry out to about 5 mm thick and use biscuit cutters to cut out different shapes, such as stars, angels and Christmas trees. Arrange on trays lined with greaseproof paper. Bake in the oven for 5–7 minutes, or until the biscuits start to colour. Cool on a rack.

Leave the biscuits plain or, if you like, decorate them with an icing made of icing sugar and a few drops of lemon juice. You can give the angels faces, hair and dresses, and decorate the Christmas trees – just use your imagination!

Store the biscuits in an airtight jar or biscuit tin.

Vanille Kipferl

Makes about 30–40 biscuits

250 g ground almonds

250 g unsalted butter,
  at room temperature

270 g unbleached plain flour

150 g caster sugar

pinch of salt

1½ teaspoons pure
  vanilla extract

icing sugar, for dusting

Mix all the ingredients together except for the icing sugar.

Shape the dough into little crescents about 4 cm long and roughly as thick as your index finger. Arrange the biscuits on trays covered with greaseproof paper. Refrigerate for 30 minutes.

Preheat the oven to 180°C (gas mark 4).

Bake the biscuits for about 15 minutes, or until pale golden. Cool and then dust with icing sugar. Keep in an airtight jar or biscuit tin.

Birichini

Makes about 30–40 biscuits

400 g unbleached plain flour

250 g unsalted butter,
  at room temperature

100 g caster sugar

pinch of salt

raspberry jam

apricot jam

icing sugar, for dusting

Mix the flour, butter, sugar and salt together to form a dough. Shape the dough into a ball and refrigerate for about 30 minutes.

Preheat the oven to 180°C (gas mark 4).

Roll the dough out to about 5 mm thick. With a biscuit cutter, cut out circles or hearts of about 3–4 cm in diameter. Take half of these shapes and in the centre cut out smaller stars or hearts – these will become the 'lids'.

Arrange all of the biscuits on trays lined with greaseproof paper and bake in the oven for about 4 minutes. The biscuits should be very pale in colour. Cool on a rack.

Spread a little raspberry jam on some of the 'base' biscuits and apricot jam on the rest. Cover the raspberry ones with heart-shaped lids and the apricot ones with star-shaped lids. Dust the biscuits with icing sugar. Keep in an airtight jar or biscuit tin.

Caolato

Caramel Cream

Serves 8

3 organic egg yolks

pinch of salt

200 g caster sugar

500 ml cream

1 teaspoon water

This was my mother's version of crème brûlée.

I like to serve this delicious caramel-flavoured cream in small coffee cups. Your guests will expect it to be an espresso coffee, but will react with delight once they have tried the 'mystery' dessert.

In a mixing bowl, beat the egg yolks, salt and 2 tablespoons of the sugar until light and fluffy. Add the cream and beat for a further few minutes.

Heat the cream and egg mixture in a saucepan on low heat for just a few minutes.

Put the remaining sugar and the water in a saucepan over low heat and let it caramelise. Make sure the sugar does not burn.

Now add the caramel drop by drop to the cream mixture, beating vigorously with a whisk, making sure the caramel dissolves. The mixture will develop a beautiful caramel colour and thicken to a cream consistency.

Pour the cream into 8 small ramekins and refrigerate. Serve with whipped cream and biscuits on the side.

Zabaglione

Serves 4

4 organic egg yolks
120 g caster sugar
pinch of salt
200 ml Marsala

Zabaglione is one of those wonderful rich Italian desserts. I think winter is the ideal season to indulge in such luxury. The smooth, silky, sweet flavour makes you forget the frozen landscape outside.

In a mixing bowl, beat the egg yolks and sugar until they are fluffy and light in colour. Add the salt then slowly add the Marsala, whisking constantly.

Place the bowl over a saucepan of simmering water and continue whisking while the mixture gradually heats up. After about 5 minutes, the mixture will have doubled in size.

Remove from the heat (be careful not to overheat the mixture, or the eggs will scramble). Pour the zabaglione into individual glasses and serve at once, with biscuits on the side, if desired.

Ceppo di Natale

Christmas Log

Serves 6

WALNUT SPONGE

4 organic eggs, separated

75 g caster sugar

150 g walnuts, lightly
toasted and ground

1 teaspoon pure vanilla
extract

½ teaspoon salt

½ teaspoon baking powder

FILLING

250 ml cream

2 tablespoons caster sugar

reserved ground walnuts

½ teaspoon pure vanilla
extract or 3 teaspoons
Nocino liqueur

pinch of salt

ICING

icing sugar, for dusting

OR

200 g unsalted butter,
at room temperature

50 g caster sugar

3 teaspoons Nocino
liqueur or ½ teaspoon
pure vanilla extract

This wonderful roll is a traditional Christmas cake. What makes it particularly delicious are the walnuts. I like to serve it year-round. You can either dust it with icing sugar or, more authentically, ice it to look like a tree trunk.

Preheat the oven to 220°C (430°F). Line a 30 × 40 cm tray with greaseproof paper, leaving some overhanging paper at the ends.

Beat the egg yolks and sugar until light and fluffy, then fold in most of the walnuts (reserving 3 tablespoons for the filling), the vanilla and salt. Set the batter aside.

Beat the egg whites and baking powder until stiff but not dry. Gradually fold them into the sponge batter. Pour the batter into the tray and spread it out evenly. Bake the sponge in the oven for 5 minutes, or until the top is lightly golden.

When the sponge is out of the oven, take one end of the paper and slide the sponge out of the tray onto a work surface. Place the tray upside down over the sponge (the steam this creates will keep the sponge soft and pliable) and leave it to cool.

For the filling, beat the cream and sugar until stiff, then fold in the extra 3 tablespoons of walnuts, the vanilla and salt.

Flip the sponge upside down onto a fresh piece of greaseproof paper and peel off the top layer of paper. Spread the filling over the cooled sponge and roll the sponge up widthways. Wrap the roll up tightly with the paper to hold it together. Refrigerate for 2 hours.

Dust with icing sugar, slice and serve. Alternatively, mix the icing ingredients and spread it over the roll. For a wooden log effect, pull a fork in raking motions through the icing.

Monte Bianco

White Mountain

Serves 6

MERINGUES

6 organic egg whites

250 g caster sugar

pinch of salt

1 teaspoon white
wine vinegar

1 teaspoon pure
vanilla extract

CHESTNUT BASE

600 g unsweetened
chestnut purée

75 g caster sugar

50–100 ml cream

TOPPING

12 meringues (see below)

250 ml cream

3 tablespoons caster sugar

This dessert, which I find easier to make with chestnut purée rather than whole chestnuts, should look like a mountain covered in snow. (Monte Bianco is the highest mountain in the Alps.)

MERINGUES

Preheat the oven to 150°C (gas mark 2).

Beat the egg whites until they start to form peaks. Add half the sugar and a pinch of salt and continue beating until the egg whites become shiny. Add the rest of the sugar, vinegar and vanilla and continue beating a little longer.

Line a large tray with greaseproof paper. Using a soup spoon, scoop out large spoonfuls of the meringue mixture and flip them onto the tray. If you prefer you can push the mixture through a piping bag.

Put the meringues into the preheated oven, turn the heat down to 120°C (gas mark ½) and cook them for about 30 minutes. Put a wooden spoon in the oven door to keep it slightly open and continue cooking the meringues for another hour. They should be crisp on the outside but still a little soft on the inside.

Transfer them to a rack and let them cool completely.

Mix the chestnut purée with the sugar, and add just enough cream so that the chestnut mass can be pushed through a potato ricer.

On a large serving plate make a mound of chestnut 'worms' by pushing the mixture through the ricer.

For the topping, arrange the meringues around the chestnut mound to make a mountain. Beat the cream and sugar until stiff and put it into a piping bag. Pipe the cream into the gaps between the meringues.

Arance Sanguine

Blood Orange Salad

Serves 6

CARAMELISED ALMONDS

100 g sugar

10 almonds

6 blood oranges, peeled and
  cut crossways into thin
  slices

4 best-quality dates, pitted
  and cut into thin strips

1 punnet raspberries

This is a beautiful dessert – very light but full of flavour.

Put the sugar in a small saucepan and heat it gently without stirring until the sugar caramelises to a golden-brown. Now add the almonds and cook just a little longer, being careful that the sugar doesn't burn. Pour the mixture onto a tray lined with greaseproof paper and leave to cool.

When the caramel is cold, put it into a plastic bag and beat it with a meat tenderiser or rolling pin until you have small, crunchy pieces.

Arrange the oranges on a serving dish, mixing the dates through them. Heap the raspberries in the middle then sprinkle the almond crunch on top. Serve just like this, or with some mascarpone sweetened with a little sugar, if desired.

Dolce di Ricotta

Sweet Ricotta

Serves 4

4 very fresh organic egg yolks

60 g caster sugar

500 g fresh ricotta

125 ml Nocino (walnut liqueur) or vin santo (see Variation)

300 ml cream

CARAMELISED WALNUTS

80 g caster sugar

50 ml cream

12 walnut halves

Beat the egg yolks and sugar together until light and fluffy. Add the ricotta and the Nocino and mix well.

In a separate bowl, beat the cream until stiff, then fold the cream into the ricotta mixture.

Line a jelly mould (or individual moulds) with cheesecloth (muslin). Pour the ricotta mixture into the mould(s) and refrigerate for at least 4 hours or, better still, overnight.

On the day you intend to serve the ricotta, make the walnuts. Caramelise the sugar over low heat. When the sugar is golden-brown, add the cream and stir vigorously with a wooden spoon until it is well mixed (about 1–2 minutes). Now add the walnut halves and toss them in the caramel mixture until they are all well coated. Lay them out on a piece of greaseproof paper.

Unmould the ricotta onto a serving dish or, if you are using individual moulds, onto small plates. Decorate with the caramelised walnuts and serve.

Variation
If you are using vin santo, you can mix some finely grated organic lemon and orange zest into the ricotta mixture. You can then caramelise finely cut orange zest instead of the walnuts.

INDEX

conversion tables

WEIGHT

Metric	Imperial
10-15 g	½ oz
20 g	¾ oz
30 g	1 oz
40 g	1½ oz
50-60 g	2 oz
75 g	2½ oz
80 g	3 oz
100 g	3½ oz
125 g	4 oz
150 g	5 oz
175 g	6 oz
200 g	7 oz
225 g	8 oz
250 g	9 oz
275 g	10 oz
300 g	10½ oz
350 g	12 oz
400 g	14 oz
450 g	1 lb
500 g	1 lb 2 oz
600 g	1 lb 5 oz
650 g	1 lb 7 oz
750 g	1 lb 10 oz
900 g	2 lb
1 kg	2 lb 3 oz

VOLUME

Metric	Imperial
50-60 ml	2 fl oz
75 ml	2½ fl oz
100 ml	3½ fl oz
120 ml	4 fl oz
150 ml	5 fl oz
170 ml	6 fl oz
200 ml	7 fl oz
225 ml	8 fl oz
250 ml	8½ fl oz
300 ml	10 fl oz
400 ml	13 fl oz
500 ml	17 fl oz
600 ml	20 fl oz (1 pint)
750 ml	25 fl oz (1 pint 5 fl oz)
1 litre	34 fl oz (1 pint 14 fl oz)

Note: A pint in the US contains 16 fl oz;
a pint in the UK contains 20 fl oz.

TEASPOONS, TABLESPOONS & CUPS

1 teaspoon	5 ml
1 tablespoon	20 ml
1 cup	250 ml

This book uses metric cup measurements, i.e. **250 ml for 1 cup**; in the US a cup is 8 fl oz, just smaller, and **American cooks should be generous** in their cup measurements; in the UK a cup is 10 fl oz and **British cooks should be scant** with their cup measurements.

TEMPERATURE

C°	F°
140	275
150	300
160	320
170	340
180	350
190	375
200	400
210	410
220	430

LENGTH

Metric	Imperial
5 mm	¼ in
1 cm	½ in
2 cm	¾ in
2.5 cm	1 in
5 cm	2 in
7.5 cm	3 in
10 cm	4 in
15 cm	6 in
20 cm	8 in
30 cm	12 in

Acknowledgements

This book has been a long time in the making and too many people have had a helping hand in the various recipes to mention individually. Like the food itself, they have become part of the mix of wonderful ingredients that produce the finished product.

I would like to acknowledge my long-time collaborator Simon Griffiths who has taken the photographs for all my books and took more for this one too. Simon has an instinctive understanding for food, particularly my food, and this shines through in all his work.

The design team of Klarissa Pfisterer and Hamish Freeman have again contributed their special sensitivity to produce the beautiful layout and appearance of the book.

I have been helped in making the many choices needed for this book by my friend Maria Scarf.

Hardie Grant have always encouraged me to produce a book of this kind and I acknowledge Sandy Grant, whose idea it was, and Gordana Trifunovic, who, as my project editor, has worked closely with me to bring the idea to life.

Manuela